To: Dewaa

From: Daddy & Marienne

Ki Maurett

12/20

CALLED & ACCOUNTABLE

52-week Devotional

Discovering Your place
in God's Eternal purpose

CALLED &
ACCOUNTABLE
52-week Devotional

HENRY & NORMAN
BLACKABY

WITH DANA BLACKABY

NEW HOPE
PUBLISHERS

BIRMINGHAM, ALABAMA

New Hope® Publishers
P. O. Box 12065
Birmingham, AL 35202-2065
www.newhopepublishers.com

New Hope Publishers is a division of WMU®.

Library of Congress Cataloging-in-Publication Data
Blackaby, Norman C.
  Called & accountable 52-week devotional : discovering your place in
God's eternal purpose / Norman and Henry Blackaby, with Dana Blackaby.
  p. cm.
  Includes index.
  ISBN 978-1-59669-214-5 (hc)
  1. Vocation—Christianity—Meditations. 2. Devotional calendars. I.
Blackaby, Henry T., 1935- II. Blackaby, Dana. III. Title. IV. Title:
Called and accountable fifty two-week devotional.
  BV4740.B573 2007
  242'.2—dc22
    2007026918

ISBN-10: 1-59669-214-6
ISBN-13: 978-1-59669-214-5

N084137 • 1207 • 15M1

DEDICATION

To my uncle and his wife, *Lorimer and Olive Baker,*
who faithfully served as missionaries in Manchuria, China,
working with Jonathan Goforth during the great
Shantung Revival, and who baptized me as a nine-year-old boy and
later became my pastor when God called me into the ministry.
—HENRY BLACKABY

To our three children—*Emily, Douglas, and Anne*—
our fellow partners in living out God's call on our family.
—NORMAN AND DANA BLACKABY

Table of Contents

Preface

Since the release of the revised *Called and Accountable* workbook (2005) and the *Called and Accountable* trade book (2007), we have received very encouraging affirmation from people around the world. Many of God's people have shared that the truths presented in these two books have served as "refreshment" to their hearts and, in turn, helped them sense a renewed call upon their lives.

In the preface of the previous works, we stated that the message of *Called and Accountable* has been on our hearts for many years. In 1986, I [Henry] was asked to speak at a retreat in Toccoa, Georgia. This conference was of particular significance in that it shaped the direction of the rest of my ministry and the life of my family. At this retreat, I preached four sermons: "All Are Called," "All Are Gifted," "All Are Sent," and, in conclusion, "How to Hear God." I was asked to put the teachings from the last session into writing, so that session's teachings eventually became the workbook *Experiencing God: Knowing and Doing the Will of God.* The teachings of the first three sessions were put into a small 35-page book titled *Called and Accountable.* This book was turned into a workbook, which has since been enlarged and completely revised in 2005. In 2007, *Called and Accountable* was also published as a read, without workbook pages.

The purpose of this devotional is to keep the truths of *Called and Accountable* before us throughout the year. At times, we can read a book or complete a study that has a significant impact on our lives. However, as time passes, we can forget the truths that impacted us during our study. Our prayer is that the devotionals presented in this book will keep our lives grounded in the facts that we are all called to a relationship with God and that we will have to give an account for the manner in which we walked—whether our walk was worthy of this calling.

This devotional is not intended as a daily devotional, but is intended as a 52-week study. Our desire is for the reader to study one devotional per week to help keep his or her focus on God's call throughout the entire year. The material found in this devotional has been drawn from the truths discussed in the previous *Called and Accountable* books. Our hope is that this devotional will serve to reinforce the reader's sense of the call of God.

So choose a day each week to read this devotional. Then, through the week, take time to review the devotional text and address the comments and study questions in the "Digging Deeper Through the Week" section. These simple exercises will help you stay focused on the call throughout the week.

We pray that this devotional will be an encouragement to many of God's people to wholeheartedly live out God's call upon their lives. May we all strive *"to walk worthy of the calling with which [we] were called"* (Ephesians 4:1).

—HENRY BLACKABY, NORMAN BLACKABY,

AND DANA BLACKABY

Called to Be His People

*You also, as living stones, are being built
up a spiritual house, a holy priesthood, to offer
up spiritual sacrifices acceptable to God through
Jesus Christ.... But you are a chosen generation,
a royal priesthood, a holy nation, His own special
people, that you may proclaim the praises of Him
who called you out of darkness into His marvelous
light; who once were not a people but are now the
people of God, who had not obtained mercy
but now have obtained mercy.*

—1 Peter 2:5, 9–10

Who are the called? Are they a special group of persons? What about my life? Am I called too? How would I know? What would it sound like? Do these questions ever cross your mind?

Your heart may sincerely be saying, "Lord, I do love You! I do belong to You! I am Your servant, and I truly want to serve You. But am I really called to be on mission with You in my world? Lord, just who are the called?"

Unfortunately, our "Christian culture" has not always been thoroughly biblical. That is, as we have made a difference between clergy and laypeople, so we have assumed a difference between the

11

specially called and the common believer. In reality, *all believers are the called!* The difference lies not in whether all believers are called, but in the nature of the assignments given by God. But all believers are called by God, for Him to be free to accomplish His purposes in them and through them!

Let's look briefly at some Scripture passages that assure us that every believer is called. In Exodus 19, when God created a special nation through which He would bring salvation to the whole world, He said:

> *"'You have seen what I did to the Egyptians, and how I bore you on eagles' wings and brought you to Myself. Now therefore, if you will indeed obey My voice and keep My covenant, then you shall be a special treasure to Me above all people; for all the earth is Mine. And you shall be to Me a kingdom of priests and a holy nation.' These are the words which you shall speak to the children of Israel."*
>
> —EXODUS 19:4–6

Did you notice that God said they would be a *"kingdom of priests"*—not a *kingdom with a priesthood*? Each and every one of them would be priests unto God. The Levites would be the ones assigned to train and equip the entire nation to walk with God as priests unto God so He could fulfill His purposes to save the nations of the world through them. This same truth is stated in the New Testament. Notice how Paul addressed the people of the church at Rome:

> *Through Him we have received grace and apostleship for obedience to the faith among all nations for His name, among whom you also are the called of Jesus Christ.*
>
> —ROMANS 1:5–6

For what did Paul say he received grace and apostleship? Yes, it was for obedience to the faith. There is little question that those who receive salvation from God release themselves, at that same time, to the call of obedience that comes from faith. They go hand in hand. When you received Christ into your life, did you understand that, at that same moment, you were releasing your life to be used any way God would choose?

Lord, I know that You have a plan to use my life in this generation. Please make me aware today of where You are working in my home, neighborhood, church, and workplace. Make my heart ready all through the day so You can use me. Amen.

DIGGING DEEPER
THROUGH THE WEEK

Read the Book of Esther this week. By most definitions of society in that day, Esther was a "nobody." She was an orphan, a woman, and an exile. Yet she was called of God and used by God to save His children in her generation.

All believers are called to be on mission with God. Do you realize that you were placed in the world in this generation for *"such a time as this"* (see Esther 4:14)? What assignment has God given you? Consider throughout this week: Are you faithfully living each day as a priest unto God?

As you work through these "Digging Deeper Through the Week" sections, record your thoughts and questions and *God's responses* in a journal.

Called to Abide in Him

"If you keep My commandments, you will abide in My love, just as I have kept My Father's commandments and abide in His love."

—John 15:10

In the mind and heart of God, so much is at stake when He calls a person! His call to us is not merely so we can go to heaven when we die, but so we can begin knowing Him, walking with Him, and serving Him from the time of salvation on and throughout eternity. He desires a relationship with those He calls—a *love relationship*! Jesus is the pattern of love for us. God first loved us, drew us to Himself, adopted us into His family through salvation, and sent the Holy Spirit to reside in us so that we could experience and share His love with others.

In John 15:1–8, Jesus paints a picture showing that He is the Vine and we are the branches. Sometimes we may imagine the vine as nothing more than the stem, but the vine consists of the roots, stem, branches, leaves, and fruit. The vine is everything. The Apostle Paul describes this abiding as being *"in Christ"* and that is why he could say, *"To live is Christ"* (Philippians 1:21). To abide in Him is to release our lives to Him so He can shape and transform each area of our lives. To abide in His love is to let the relationship

14

of love permeate every aspect of our lives. This love relationship will grow as we read and live out the Scriptures, spend time in prayer, grow in fellowship with other Christians, and join God in service and ministry.

The evidence that we are abiding in His love is that we find ourselves obeying His commands (John 15:10). This is not referring to a legalistic or harsh obedience, but a natural desire to follow and obey our Lord's commands out of love. Jesus tells us that as we obey Him from this love relationship, the result will be that we remain in His love in the same way that He remains in the heavenly Father's love. He explains further that if we do these things, His joy will remain in us to its fullest capacity (v. 11). When we obey Him, we will abide in His love, and we will experience His joy to the fullest measure.

Jesus describes a new relationship He develops with His disciples as they learn to obey:

> *"You are My friends if you do whatever I command you. No longer do I call you servants, for a servant does not know what his master is doing; but I have called you friends, for all things that I heard from My Father I have made known to you."*
>
> —JOHN 15:14–15

Notice how Jesus describes this new love relationship. Jesus says that the ones who keep His commandments will no longer be called His servants or slaves, but they will be called His friends. He goes on to describe this intimate friendship by saying He will reveal all things that He hears from His Father to the ones who keep His commands and abide in His love (vv. 10, 15).

How would you describe your obedience to Jesus? Prayerfully reflect on the past week or month. Ask yourself, "What have I heard from my Lord?" and "Have I made the necessary adjustments in my life to obey everything He has told me?"

 Heavenly Father, I know that without You, I can do nothing. Keep me in close fellowship with You through Your Holy Spirit, and use my life to accomplish Your plans today.

DIGGING DEEPER
THROUGH THE WEEK

Spend time this week reading John 15. Read it several times, and ask the Lord to teach you what it means to abide in the Vine. Ask Him to show you a picture of the relationship you have with Him. Ask Him to examine your obedience to His commands and to show you if you are walking in obedience to all He has instructed you to do and say.

Jesus states that He knows God's children really love Him because they obey Him. Consider Jesus's conversation with Peter in John 21:15–19. Jesus came to Peter after he had denied Jesus and challenged Peter to press on in obedience. If God has convicted you of disobedience, be quick to show your love for Him by repenting of this sin and returning to Him. Let Him restore the love relationship!

Called to Be God's Instrument

*He chose us in Him before the foundation of
the world, that we should be holy and without
blame before Him in love.*

—Ephesians 1:4

The entire Bible bears witness to the truth that God, from eternity, chose to work through His people to accomplish His eternal purposes in the world. He could have worked out everything by Himself, just as He worked during the Creation, but He chose not to do it that way. Rather, the Bible tells how God called individuals into a special relationship with Himself so that He could use them to accomplish His purposes.

When God was about to destroy every living thing from the earth because of sin, He called Noah to Himself and, through Noah, preserved his family and enough living creatures to begin to populate the earth again (Genesis 6–10). When God wanted to establish saving faith (salvation) for all mankind, He chose Abram, whose name He changed to Abraham, to be the one He would shape to be a sample of that faith to the end of time (Genesis 12–22; Hebrews 11:8). When God was ready to deliver His chosen people from bondage in Egypt, He called Moses to Himself and sent him to be the one through whom He would accomplish this task (Exodus 3).

The New Testament is filled with examples of God choosing people to be used to accomplish His purposes. The choosing of the Twelve and the call of the Apostle Paul are the most obvious examples.

A quick look at church history reveals numerous examples of God calling out and using people to bring about His purposes. When, in God's timing, He desired the Bible to be translated into the common language of the English-speaking world, He raised up William Tyndale for the task. There was a time when God's people had moved away from the understanding and role of grace in the Christian life. At that time, God chose to impact radically the life of Martin Luther to call the people back to a salvation by grace, through faith. When God's people had lost sight of the truth that God is a God who hears and answers prayer, He called out George Müller to a ministry to orphans that would impact the world through the examples of faithfulness to prayer and God's answer and provision.

We can read the examples in Scripture and often not make the connection to our own lives. It is easy to look at the people described in Scripture and see them as larger than life. We can forget that at the time when God called these people, they were ordinary people who simply had a heart that was obedient to God when He called. The people God called were carpenters, fishermen, farmers, shepherds, servants, and businesspeople. Looking at them after God accomplished His work through their lives, we do not see them this way, but they would have seen themselves as very ordinary in their day.

Does God need us to accomplish His work? Certainly not! However, God has determined to involve His people. He calls individuals He can empower to be the instruments through which He will accomplish His eternal purposes.

*Heavenly Father, as I consider the way You choose
to work through Your children, I ask that You
use me in my generation to accomplish Your plans.
Draw me close to You, open my eyes to see where
You are working around me, and help me
to be ready to obey today. Amen.*

Digging Deeper
THROUGH THE WEEK

Read the following passages, and then answer the questions. You may want to record your thoughts in a journal.

1. Abraham—Genesis 12–13

2. Zechariah and Elizabeth—Luke 1:5–25

3. Philip—Acts 8:26–40

   • What were these people doing before God called them?

   • How was the call unique to each individual?

   • What tasks did God call them to do?

   • How did they respond?

Can you see any area in which God is calling you out for His purposes? How might you respond?

God Calls Ordinary People

*Then Amos answered, and said to Amaziah:
"I was no prophet, nor was I a son of
a prophet, but I was a sheepbreeder and a tender
of sycamore fruit. Then the LORD took me as
I followed the flock, and the LORD said to
me, 'Go, prophesy to My people Israel.'"*

—Amos 7:14–15

It is encouraging to read throughout the Bible that most of the people God called and worked through mightily were what we today would call *everyday believers*. God called and enabled them to work with Him in their world. Their abilities or skills were not as important as their relationship with God. Their heart relationship of love and trust in God always determined how much God was able to do through them. David was a shepherd, and God chose him for a special assignment: God would guide His people through him. Amos described himself this way: "I am not a prophet or son of a prophet—just a sheepbreeder." Peter was a fisherman. He and all the other disciples were what we would call just *ordinary people*—until God assigned them roles in His kingdom where He would work through them mightily to accomplish His purposes.

Let's take a look at some other ordinary people in the Scriptures whom God called and used in extravagant ways.

In Joshua 2:1, the Bible describes Rahab as a harlot. However, if we follow Rahab's life, we see that God used her life to accomplish His purposes for Israel. Rahab and her whole family were saved when God gave the city of Jericho to Israel. She was an *ordinary person* who recognized God's activity in His people (Joshua 2:9–11), and God used her life in extraordinary ways. Notice in Matthew 1:5 in the genealogy of Jesus that Rahab is listed as the mother of Boaz. She is also described in Hebrews 11:31 and James 2:25 as a woman of faith and of works.

Luke, described as a physician in Colossians 4:14, accompanied the Apostle Paul in his missionary tour of Asia and Macedonia (see Acts 16:10–13, when Luke joined Paul, and Acts 20:5–6) and on his trips to Jerusalem (Acts 21:1–18) and Rome (Acts 27–28; 2 Timothy 4:11; Philemon 24). God called a doctor, made him a disciple, and sent him into service. When you read about all that happened to Paul, can you see why God would place a doctor with him on his travels (2 Corinthians 11:24–27)?

How ordinary is your life compared with God's special assignment for you? He chooses the ordinary and the ones the world would not choose, so that when He has completed His work, He alone will receive the glory. The key is not our talents but the cultivating of our hearts, so when God does work through us, we offer the praise to Him and let others know it was God who accomplished the work. In this, God is greatly honored and His name glorified because everyone recognizes that *He did it*!

Heavenly Father, I thank You that You use
ordinary people to accomplish Your work; I feel so
 very ordinary. Please help me to be ready the moment
You come to me with an assignment, and give me the
faith I need moment by moment to obey. Amen.

Digging Deeper
THROUGH THE WEEK

Prayerfully consider where God has invited you to join Him recently. Has He revealed any hurting people to you in your workplace? Do you have a neighbor who is in a crisis? What about a family member who is in the middle of a financial dilemma?

If God brought some individuals to mind, set aside some time this week to pray for them. Ask God to use your life to bring encouragement to them.

CALLED FOR HIS PLAN

*I beseech you therefore, brethren, by the mercies
of God, that you present your bodies a living
sacrifice, holy, acceptable to God, which is your
reasonable service. And do not be conformed to
this world, but be transformed by the renewing
of your mind, that you may prove what is that
good and acceptable and perfect will of God.*

—ROMANS 12:1–2

One of the most significant illustrations of hearing and responding to God is found in the life of Mary, Jesus's mother. God's eternal purpose was to bring a Savior into the world and, through that Savior, to bring His great salvation to every person. He found the one through whom He would choose to work—Mary, a young girl. An angel announced to her God's plan to use her for His purpose. Then came her amazing and wonderful response: *"Behold the maidservant of the Lord! Let it be to me according to your word"* (Luke 1:38). And God did what He said He would do! It was impossible for mankind, but possible with God (Luke 1:37). Mary had a heart that was open toward God, and God showed Himself strong on her behalf. *"For the eyes of the LORD run to and fro throughout the whole earth, to shew himself strong in the behalf of them whose heart*

23

is perfect toward him" (2 Chronicles 16:9 KJV). This has been God's strategy from the beginning—and still is with each of us today.

There are times when we are not given any details of God's plans for our lives except that He calls us to follow Him. In these situations, our hearts have to respond as did the heart of Levi (Matthew) in Luke 5:27–29. Jesus simply walked by Levi's tax booth and asked him to follow. No details were given, but we can assume Levi knew who Jesus was and had heard all of the rumors of the teachings, preaching, and healings He had done. Levi knew enough that when the Lord called, he responded immediately: *"He left all, rose up, and followed Him"* (Luke 5:28). We see this truth clearly in the life of Abraham. God spoke to Abraham, saying, *"Get out of your country, from your family and from your father's house, to a land that I will show you"* (Genesis 12:1). And we see Abraham's response: *"So Abram departed as the LORD had spoken to him"* (Genesis 12:4). Noah is another example of an ordinary person who was faithful to follow God in his generation. He is described as *"a just man, perfect in his generations"* and a man who *"walked with God"* (Genesis 6:9). It is not surprising that Noah was ready to obey when God came to him and said, *"Make yourself an ark of gopherwood"* (Genesis 6:14). Noah's obedience saved his life and the lives of those in his family.

God works today the same way He worked in the past as recorded in the Scriptures. He presents a portion of His will to us and then waits for us to respond. We must step forward by faith, yielding our will to His and obeying His words. Then God will show us the next step we are to take, and the one after that, and so on. God won't show us the second step until, by faith, we agree and obey the first step.

God chooses to work through His people to accomplish His eternal purpose. Have you arranged your life so when God comes to you, you are ready and available to Him (presenting your life a living sacrifice)? If you would have to respond, "No, my life is not really in order to be used," then take time now to ask God to show you what changes you need to make to be available for His call on your life.

 Heavenly Father, as You work through ordinary people to accomplish things of eternal value, make my life useful to You today. Amen.

DIGGING DEEPER
THROUGH THE WEEK

God invites His children to join Him in His work today. As you read the following passages this week, pay attention to how each person responded to God's invitation. You may want to focus on one each day and record your thoughts in a journal.

1. Mary—Luke 1:26–38

2. Joshua—Joshua 1

3. Rich young ruler—Matthew 19:16–22

4. Peter—Luke 5:1–11

5. Nehemiah—Nehemiah 1–2

One hindrance we see that keeps people from being ready to go when God calls is in the area of personal finances. Debt can keep a person from feeling free to follow God when He calls.

Are your finances in order so you could obey immediately if God were to give you an assignment today?

Called to an Eternal Perspective

*And whatever you do, do it heartily, as to the
Lord and not to men, knowing that from the Lord
you will receive the reward of the inheritance;
for you serve the Lord Christ.*

—Colossians 3:23–24

In understanding the call of God, it is important to look at our lives and the world around us from God's perspective rather than through our own limited understanding. When God created us, He did not make us for time, but for eternity. As we get caught up in the events of the day or the planning of our week, it can be easy to forget this important truth. We were created in His image; this includes immortality, which means living for eternity.

As Christians, we know that when our earthly bodies die, we will spend eternity in heaven, but we often do not live as though we believe this truth. The Scriptures compare our lives on this earth to a vapor (James 4:14) or to the flowers and grass, which are here today and gone tomorrow (Isaiah 40:6–8; Matthew 6:30). When comparing our lives on this earth with our lives in heaven, the first is only a brief moment compared with an eternity. Because of this truth, upon what should we be placing our focus and energy?

How much energy and time are we spending preparing for life in heaven?

As we have asked Christians these questions over the years, very few can share how they are investing in heavenly treasures (Matthew 6:19–21). When we press it a bit further and make the comparison between the time spent preparing for our retirement on earth as opposed to the one in heaven, it becomes apparent that many Christians have not thought through the fact that they were created for eternity. We know this fact in our heads, but our actions often reveal that the truth has never settled in our hearts. John 3:16 says, *"For God so loved the world that He gave His only begotten Son, that whoever believes in Him should not perish but have everlasting life."* The key word in this verse is *perish*. As a Christian, living in the middle of a perishing world, we are called to be salt and light (Matthew 5:13–16). God makes us salt and uses us as a preserving agent in the middle of a decaying world. He uses us as light to show those around us the way to heaven through a relationship with Jesus. Our purpose on earth is to become intimately acquainted with our Lord and to live in such a way that others will want to know Him.

Certainly it is important to invest and plan for our retirement upon this earth. With so many people living into their 90s these days, financial planning is needed for the later years of life. Yet what is a 20- to 30-year retirement compared with eternity? A vapor!

 *Heavenly Father, set my mind on things above—
things of eternal value. May my investments on this
earth be founded with eternity in mind. Amen.*

DIGGING DEEPER
THROUGH THE WEEK

Think about this past week, considering how you invested your time. Make a list of the major activities you participated in, then place check marks beside the things you did that have eternal value. Time invested in people has eternal significance. Ask God if He is inviting you to encourage or disciple any certain persons. Write down their names, and ask God how you can minister to them this next week.

Matthew 6:19–21 describes how Christians are to invest in eternity. Take time to prayerfully meditate on this passage.

As you read the following passages, determine for each person named whether he or she was investing in things of eternal value.

1. Paul—Philippians 1:19–30

2. Ananias and Sapphira—Acts 5:1–11

3. Philemon—the Book of Philemon

ACCOUNTABLE FOR OBEDIENCE

*Who [Christ], in the days of His flesh, when
He had offered up prayers and supplications,
with vehement cries and tears to Him who was
able to save Him from death, and was heard
because of His godly fear, though He was
a Son, yet He learned obedience by the things
which He suffered. And having been perfected,
He became the author of eternal salvation
to all who obey Him.*

—HEBREWS 5:7–9

God's goal for each believer is for the person *"to be conformed to the image of His Son"* (Romans 8:29). *Image* can be understood as "characteristics." In other words, God is seeking to develop the character of His Son, Jesus, in each of us. As God does this in our lives, we become better instruments for use in His kingdom work.

One of the characteristics of Jesus is His faithful obedience to do exactly what the Father asks of Him. John's Gospel clearly describes this truth. For example, in John 5:19, we see Jesus explaining His actions: *"Most assuredly, I say to you, the Son can do nothing of Himself, but what He sees the Father do; for whatever He does, the Son also does in like manner."* Further, John recorded Jesus saying this:

29

> *"My doctrine is not Mine, but His who sent Me. If anyone wants to do His will, he shall know concerning the doctrine, whether it is from God or whether I speak on My own authority. He who speaks from himself seeks his own glory; but He who seeks the glory of the One who sent Him is true, and no unrighteousness is in Him."*
>
> —JOHN 7:16–18

In these passages, we see the character of our Lord clearly:
- Jesus obeyed the Father in every area of His life.
- He did only what the Father told Him to do.
- He spoke only when the Father told Him to speak.
- He taught only what the Father told Him to teach.

Remember that God desires this same obedience in our lives. God is seeking to develop the character of His Son in us. Such character is developed through our relationship with Him as He works out in our lives His eternal plan of redemption. He calls us into a relationship with Himself so, in that relationship, we can come to know His will and understand His ways and experience His working in us and through us. In that relationship, and only there, does He develop our character.

As God's people are obedient to make their lives available to God in the same way His Son was available to Him, God will work through them to accomplish His eternal purposes. The ultimate result of Christ's obedience was that the Father brought eternal salvation to the human race through the Son.

As you consider Jesus's faithful obedience to do all that the Father commanded, prayerfully reflect on your life. Can you say, as Jesus did, "I do nothing of myself, but only what I hear and see My Father doing"?

*Lord Jesus, show me where You are working
in my world. Help me to learn from You and
follow Your example of humble obedience,
even during difficult times. Amen.*

Digging Deeper
THROUGH THE WEEK

God will develop our character in the same way He developed the character of Jesus. He will mold us and shape us through circumstances, and He will allow us to learn obedience through the things that we suffer (see Hebrews 5:8).

Take a moment to examine the following passages, and consider the outcome of each situation in light of each person's character being changed. (Another way to describe "character being changed" is "faith being strengthened" through suffering.)

1. Peter—Matthew 14:22–33

2. Daniel—Daniel 6

3. Esther—Esther 3–8

4. Abraham and Isaac—Genesis 22:1–14

CALLED TO LISTEN AND RESPOND

*"He who belongs to God hears what God says.
The reason you do not hear is that you do not
belong to God."*

—JOHN 8:47 (NIV)

One must believe that God really does speak to us in this matter of His call. From Genesis through Revelation, no truth stands out any clearer than that *God speaks to His people.* They always know that it is God, they know what He is saying, and they know how they are to respond. In other words, God's speaking to His people is not simply an academic exercise or merely a theological truth. It is a real relationship with God, and He actually does call each of us to Himself for His eternal purposes.

God takes the initiative to come to His people and to let them know what He is doing or about to do. He came to Noah when He was about to judge the world by a flood. Unless God had come to him, Noah could not have known what was about to happen. But Noah did know, because God wanted to accomplish His purpose through Noah. So God gave Noah an assignment, and Noah responded as a co-worker with God.

When God was about to free His people from slavery in Egypt, He took the initiative to come to Moses and let Moses know what

He was about to do. This revelation was God's invitation for Moses to work with Him to accomplish His purposes for His people.

In the cases of Peter, James, John, and Matthew (Levi), we see them immediately forsake all and follow Jesus when invited (Luke 5:1–11, 27–28). They were not given specific instructions as to what they would be doing; they were just told to join Jesus—to come with Him.

Jeremiah was given more details as to what God had in mind for his life. He was given the difficult assignment to deliver an unpopular message to the people of Judah. The people of Jeremiah's day had continually rejected God's commands as well as the words from His prophets. Jeremiah's ministry would reveal the hardness of heart of the people, and the prophet would face much ridicule and hardship to live out the call of God on his life. God knew what Jeremiah would face as he lived out this assignment, and that is why the strong words and details were given to the prophet. God took the initiative to call Jeremiah but also provided him with the message and the assurance to live out the call.

Jeremiah came to be known as the weeping prophet because of the burden of the message he was given to share and the hardships he experienced. The disciples had to face all kinds of hardships and persecution as they shared the good news of salvation through Jesus. Throughout history, this pattern has been seen when God was about to do a great work in our world, and it is still the pattern used today. This is true right now for your life also! He chose you with an eternal purpose in mind: to use your life to make an impact on your generation and the generations to come.

*Dear Lord, as I walk through this week encountering
various circumstances, help me to view them from
Your heavenly perspective. Make me an instrument
for Your use in this generation. Amen.*

DIGGING DEEPER
THROUGH THE WEEK

When God speaks to one of His children, His message is always unique to that person. Further, the person is always sure of what God said. Such are encounters with God!

That God speaks to His children is certain. Our response to Him is crucial. What has God been saying to you through His Word and through prayer this week? Have the circumstances in your life caused you to change the direction of your prayers? Recognize that God is speaking to you and that you must respond obediently.

Accountable to Disciple

"As You sent Me into the world, I also have sent them into the world. And for their sakes I sanctify Myself, that they also may be sanctified by the truth."

—John 17:18–19

Throughout the Bible, God called many people to Himself. In the lives of each person He called, we see the eternal purpose of God unfolding. The disciples whom Jesus called to Himself provide a clear example. As Jesus called His disciples, He said, *"Follow Me."* And they immediately left all and followed Him (Matthew 4:19–20; 9:9). As we consider the way Jesus related to the disciples, we must understand and apply two key truths to our lives.

First, Jesus knew that each of His disciples had been given to Him by the Father. As He prayed in the garden of Gethsemane at the close of His physical life on earth, He affirmed it this way:

> *"I have manifested Your name to the men whom You have given Me out of the world. They were Yours, You gave them to Me, and they have kept Your word. Now they have known that all things which You have given Me are from You. For I have given to them the words which You have given Me; and*

they have received them, and have known surely that I came
forth from You; and they have believed that You sent Me."
—JOHN 17:6–8

Second, Jesus knew absolutely that one of His assignments from the Father was to prepare these believers for the Father's eternal purpose. That purpose was for the good news of His great salvation to be taken to the ends of the earth. Fulfillment of this purpose would occur after Jesus completed a critical assignment—reconciling the world to God through Jesus's death on the Cross, the Resurrection, and the Ascension.

For the entire three and one-half years of Jesus's ministry, He prepared the disciples. He took them with Him as He taught, preached, and healed. He revealed to them the Father and the Father's plans and purposes—and the disciples believed. As Jesus returned to the Father, He sent the disciples into the world in the same way the Father had sent Him into the world (John 17:18; John 20:21). He promised to give the *"keys of the kingdom of heaven"* into their hands (Matthew 16:19). They would be working with the Father and the Son, in the power of the Holy Spirit, to fulfill the Father's purpose to redeem a lost world to Himself.

This was the Father's way and is still the Father's way in each of our lives when we believe in His Son, Jesus Christ. The Father calls us to His Son and gives us to Him. As the disciples obeyed the Lord in this relationship of love, God, through them, turned their world upside down (Acts 17:6). All through history, God has continued to call and give believers to His Son to prepare them as followers, and He desires once again in our generation to do this same work of love.

Dear God, conform my life to the image of Jesus
Christ and use me today to accomplish Your purposes
in my family, my workplace, my neighborhood,
and my church. Amen.

DIGGING DEEPER
THROUGH THE WEEK

Has Jesus entrusted specific persons to you? Have you been faithful to help them grow to maturity in their relationship with Jesus Christ?

Spend time this week praying for those God has entrusted to you. Ask God to show you how to encourage them in their relationship with Him. Are there specific activities or tools God wants you to share? Ask God to guide you, according to His timing, as you seek to encourage the ones He has entrusted to you (Proverbs 25:11). Pray for the time, the methods, the tools, and the outcome of your discipling work.

ACCOUNTABLE FOR FRUITFUL LIVING

*"I am the vine, you are the branches. He who
abides in Me, and I in him, bears much fruit;
for without Me you can do nothing."*

—JOHN 15:5

Jesus said that He is the Vine and we are the branches and that we can do nothing without Him. Many times we confuse "good things" with fruit. Spiritual fruit is something that has God's fingerprints on it. It is the result of the activity of God working through His children to accomplish His purposes.

When you read the testimonies of those in the Bible and in history who have described their relationship with God, they usually tell of the overwhelming *relationship of love* that took place when they were called of God. This "call" of God is to every believer. The essence of the call is to an intimate and life-giving relationship with God, which is totally life transforming and ultimately world changing.

God chooses us so that our lives will bear fruit. At times, it may be hard to understand what fruit looks like in us. Certainly a good place to start would be Galatians 5:22–23: *"But the fruit of the Spirit is love, joy, peace, longsuffering, kindness, goodness, faithfulness, gentleness, self-control."* As God calls you and begins to work in your life so that He can use you, you should see these characteristics growing in your life.

Our lives should be producing other kinds of fruit along with those listed in Galatians. For example, in Colossians 1:10, Paul describes the fruit of good works and growing *"in the knowledge of God"*; and in Philippians 1:11, he mentions fruits of righteousness, which the *Amplified Bible* explains as *"right standing with God and right doing,"* which glorify God.

James portrays wisdom from above as bearing good fruit: it is *"first pure, then peaceable, gentle, willing to yield, full of mercy and good fruits, without partiality and without hypocrisy."* He goes on to say that peaceful people bear *righteousness* as fruit (James 3:17–18).

When God chose us, He also designed our lives to bear good fruit. This fruit includes our character as well as our service to God in His work. With the strong emphasis that Jesus placed on bearing fruit (Luke 13:6–9), it is important to look and see what your life is yielding.

One of the most obvious characteristics that indicates your life is bearing fruit is that God is glorified. Is God doing work in your life that can only be described as "His activity"? If so, He is bearing fruit through you, and He will receive the glory.

Dear Lord, I want You to be pleased when You look at my life. Show me where You are working and how I can join You so that You can bear fruit through me this week. Amen.

Digging Deeper

If persons close to you (spouse, co-worker, pastor, or friend) were to describe your life in Christ, how would they describe it? Would they say, "Without God, he [or she] can do nothing"? Or would they say, "Without God, she [or he] cannot do very much"? Maybe they would describe your life like this, "Without God, he [or she] can do most things."

The Bible describes the "fruit" that should be evident in the life of a child of God. Do you see this fruit growing in your life? In what areas of your private and public life do you see fruitfulness? How does this fruitfulness line up with God's Word in the following passages?

1. Luke 13:6–9

2. Galatians 5:22–23

3. Philippians 1:11

4. Colossians 1:10

5. James 3:17–18

CALLED TO ADJUST

*So when they had brought their boats to land,
they forsook all and followed Him.*

—LUKE 5:11

The call of God will always involve some kind of major adjustment in your life in order for you to be the person God can use to accomplish His purposes. Moses had to leave herding sheep to lead God's people. David could not be a shepherd and be king at the same time. The disciples of Jesus could not continue their fishing and follow Jesus to learn to become fishers of men.

One of the greatest developments today is the tremendous number of missions volunteers who are leaving all and following Jesus—across North America and around the world. Teachers are going to China, as well as to other nations, so our Lord can reach people in those nations through them. Businesspeople are making their lives available through their business connections around the world so Christ can bring to Himself lost persons who would not hear any other way. Each year, tens of thousands of volunteers are going around the world with a deep sense of being on mission with the Lord. What a difference this is making in our generation!

God's call requires only one response from every believer—obedience! Once you, as a child of God, recognize the activity of God in your life, you must immediately, without resistance or discussion, respond obediently to all God is directing. Only then will you experience God's working mightily through your life. At times, we tend to take our obedience to God lightly. However, God views our obedience as an essential key to our relationship with Him.

Let's look at a few examples in the Scriptures. As you read these verses, pay careful attention to how God views our obedience or disobedience to Him.

"If you love Me, keep My commandments."

—JOHN 14:15

Jesus answered and said to him, "If anyone loves Me, he will keep My word; and My Father will love him, and We will come to him and make Our home with him. He who does not love Me does not keep My words; and the word which you hear is not Mine but the Father's who sent Me."

—JOHN 14:23–24

So Samuel said: "Has the LORD as great delight in burnt offerings and sacrifices, as in obeying the voice of the LORD? Behold, to obey is better than sacrifice, and to heed than the fat of rams."

—1 SAMUEL 15:22

For many, the greatest challenge is not that they *do not know* the will of God, but rather that they *do know* His will but *have not been willing* to make the necessary adjustments to obey Him! Jesus's love for us was settled on the Cross. Our love for Jesus is expressed daily through our obedience to Him. The Father sees our love for Him when we have an obedient heart. Obedience is always the key to experiencing a life on mission with God in our world!

What about your life? Are you hearing a word from God, immediately obeying Him, and experiencing God working through your life each day? Do you stop to recognize how God accomplishes His work through your obedience? Are you seeing things happen in your life that can only be described as the activity of God?

Dear Lord, give me eyes to see where You are working and ears to hear what You are saying to me this week. And please make my heart ready to obey immediately. Amen.

DIGGING DEEPER
THROUGH THE WEEK

Many times people are afraid to respond to God's call because they feel it will cost them or their family too much. Some people want to obey on their own terms—or negotiate with God based on their best thinking. We call this "partial obedience," which is really disobedience.

Read the following Scriptures, and notice how each person's obedience or disobedience affected his or her life and future ministry.

1. Moses—Numbers 20:6–12; Deuteronomy 34:1–12

2. Saul—1 Samuel 15

3. The disciples—Luke 5:1–11

4. The women who served Jesus along with the disciples—Luke 8:1–3

CALLED TO HIS ASSIGNMENT

*He sent them to preach the kingdom of God
and to heal the sick.*

—LUKE 9:2

It is an awesome truth to understand that the God of the universe calls us to be on mission with Him in our world. When He calls us, He is inviting us to follow Him. Accepting His invitation requires us to make adjustments in our lives. As God transforms us, He lays His heart over ours, and we begin to share His burden—that He is *"not willing that any should perish but that all should come to repentance"* (2 Peter 3:9). God, who sent His only Son into the world that we *"through Him might be saved"* (John 3:16–17), will also send us into the world that others might be saved by our witness to His great salvation.

In order to be on mission with God, we must have a heart that responds, "Yes, Lord," each time we hear a whisper from Him. This truth, again, is seen throughout the Bible, and those mightily used throughout history bear witness to its reality.

From the moment of salvation, there comes over the new believer a deep sense of being on mission with the Lord in the world. Some people indicate that at salvation they sensed a call to missions, evangelism, and/or witnessing. This is normal for every new believer.

The longer we walk with God, the more we will become like Him. He will give us His heart for the world. You see, it is impossible to live intimately with God and not be *"transformed into the same image from glory to glory, just as by the Spirit of the Lord"* (2 Corinthians 3:18). In Philippians 2:5–11, Paul urged the believers in the church at Philippi to accept the mind of Christ— *"Let this mind be in you which was also in Christ Jesus"* (v. 5)—and then identified what this would mean specifically. He expected the mind of Christ to be formed in them, so he urged them to let it happen.

Hebrews 13:20–21 shows us that God desires to equip and enable believers with everything needed for doing His will. Each believer must let the full implications of salvation work into every area of life. Each Christian must respond to Him as Lord over all of his or her life, for it is He who will be working in the life of the believer, causing that person to *want* to do His will, and then working in that life to *enable* the person to do it. What an exciting invitation for every believer!

Heavenly Father, I want to be ready to follow and obey You when You speak to me. When You give me assignments this week and in the weeks to come, may I always immediately respond, "Yes, Lord." Amen.

DIGGING DEEPER
THROUGH THE WEEK

As you look back over the past few months or years, you probably recognize many times when God invited you to be on mission with Him. What changes has your obedience to follow Him caused you to make? (You might think of this in terms of your family, workplace, community, or church.) What fears have you needed to overcome?

As you pray, ask God to show you areas in which He is inviting you to join Him this week. What adjustments will you need to make to join Him in His activity?

When we are faced with a new assignment, often our first response is fear. Fear must be replaced with faith. Fear will cause you to stumble; faith will enable you to complete the assignment. When fear is present, you must trust God to do what is best. Look back over your life and ask God to remind you of all of the ways He has taken care of you and shown mercy to you time and time again.

This week, make a list of all the ways God has carried you through difficult or uncertain circumstances in your lifetime. Keep your list in a place where you can add to it throughout this week. Remember the goodness of God as you approach a new assignment; this will bring joy to your heart as you obey by faith!

CALLED TO HIS TIMETABLE

"Has the LORD as great delight in burnt offerings and sacrifices, as in obeying the voice of the LORD? Behold, to obey is better than sacrifice, and to heed than the fat of rams."

—1 SAMUEL 15:22

Every Christian is called to be on mission with God in the world (Matthew 28:19–20). This is what it means to be called. God is seeking to bring a lost world back to Himself. He loves every person, and He is not willing that any should perish. He has always been working in this world to seek and to save those who are lost. That is what He was doing when He called you! Those He saves, He involves as fellow workers with Himself in His eternal purpose to save a lost world.

Looking back to the day of your salvation, can you see that God began working through your life at that moment? On that day, He began to open your understanding to His plans to use your life in your generation. He planned to use your life to have an impact on your family, friends, co-workers, and church family for eternity.

Our response to God's invitation to join Him in His work is crucial. A wonderful example of this truth is seen in the life of Joseph, the one who fulfilled the role of earthly father for Jesus.

Take a moment to read Matthew 1:18 through 2:23. As you read, take note of Joseph's role in the birth of Jesus and specifically consider his obedience.

What was God about to do when He came to Joseph? He was about to bring salvation to the world.

Did you notice how quickly Joseph obeyed each time God spoke to him? Can you imagine what the outcome could have been had he not recognized God's instructions and stepped out in faith quickly? His choice of whether to obey was an issue of life or death for his family! His immediate obedience saved the life of the special Child in his care and fulfilled prophecy.

In the same way, when God speaks to us, the timing is critical, and the lives of those closest to us may depend on our faith and quick obedience. When God gives us an assignment, we can trust that His timing is perfect!

Has God instructed you to do something recently? How did you respond? Did you recognize the importance of the timing of God's instructions as they fit into His eternal plans? Take some time now to pray and ask God if He has given any instruction to which you have not responded.

If God brings to mind some areas in which you have not obeyed, write them down, and ask the Lord to help you adjust your life immediately to His will.

  Dear Lord, thank You for the example of Joseph's life and his immediate obedience. I realize that my obedience to You must be the same. Please give me wisdom to follow and obey Your every word today. Amen.

DIGGING DEEPER
THROUGH THE WEEK

Take time this week to read and study the account of Jesus's birth and first two years of His life in Matthew 1:18 through 2:23. Notice how God spoke to Joseph and his immediate obedience. His obedience was a matter of life or death to his family. Our obedience is no different. We must take seriously every word God speaks to us and be quick to obey.

Called to Persevere

> *"For the eyes of the LORD run to and fro*
> *throughout the whole earth, to show Himself strong*
> *on behalf of those whose heart is loyal to Him."*
>
> —2 Chronicles 16:9

Each one of us is important to God! We are ordinary people who love God with all our hearts and know that the call to salvation is also a call to be laborers together with God in our world. As we respond to the call of God and yield to Him, He powerfully accomplishes His purpose to save a lost world through our lives. God seeks out those who are willing to stand before Him on behalf of the land:

> *"So I sought for a man among them who would make a wall, and stand in the gap before Me on behalf of the land, that I should not destroy it; but I found no one. Therefore I have poured out My indignation on them; I have consumed them with the fire of My wrath; and I have recompensed their deeds on their own heads," says the Lord GOD.*
>
> —Ezekiel 22:30–31

If God does not find a person to *"stand in the gap,"* the land and the people are destroyed. But when He does find someone who will willingly obey every word He speaks—do the job—He is able to save multitudes of people.

When God knew Nineveh was ready to repent, He called Jonah to stand in the gap.

When Jonah finally obeyed God's assignment to take His message to the people of the great city of Nineveh, the king and all the people responded with immediate and thorough repentance, and the entire city was saved. This was the intent of God's heart, and it waited on the obedience of an ordinary child of God. Jonah, however, was not willing to respond to God's call at first.

We may not understand *why* God chooses to use individuals and often waits on their response before He acts, but *that He chooses to work through His people is very clear*. If we have been unwilling to be the one that God could use as His instrument, then we must ask ourselves, "What could have been if only I had responded immediately to God's invitation to join Him in His heart for the lost?" We can get caught up in our own world and not recognize that the eternal lives of people hang in the balance as God waits on our response to Him.

What about your life? Has God given you an assignment that you have been "running" from? If so, let us encourage you to run to God in repentance. The safest place to be is walking in obedience to God's call.

God, please give me courage this week as I serve You. May my spiritual ears be listening for Your voice, and may my heart be ready to immediately obey Your words. In Jesus's name, Amen.

DIGGING DEEPER
THROUGH THE WEEK

Many times the assignments God gives require His children to suffer personal pain. Often we want to avoid difficult assignments because of the consequences we might face. We must look to Jesus as our example of obedience even if it means humiliation, suffering, or loss. His obedience to the Father secured our salvation—but it required Him to die an undeserved, humiliating death.

Maybe you have already obeyed the Father's assignment and found yourself in a circumstance that could be interpreted as a personal failure. Again, look to Jesus's example: He didn't look at the Cross as a personal failure. Rather, He saw it in light of God's eternal plan.

Spend time this week meditating on the Cross, and read about it in all four Gospels.

1. Matthew 26–27

2. Mark 14–15

3. Luke 22–23

4. John 18–19

Called to an Intimate Relationship

"And this is eternal life: [it means] to know
(to perceive, recognize, become acquainted with, and
understand) You, the only true and real God, and
[likewise] to know Him, Jesus [as the] Christ
(the Anointed One, the Messiah),
Whom You have sent."

—John 17:3 (AMP)

Throughout all generations, God has called His people to return to a love relationship with Him. The Bible is the story of God's redemptive love providing everyone who will believe in His Son a way back to His love. God gave salvation through His Son so that His eternal purpose of love could be restored.

Too often, people think of this salvation as simply providing a way to go to heaven at death, which is certainly a vital part of God's great salvation. However, God did not create us for time, but for eternity! It is important to keep in mind Jesus's definition of "eternal life" found in John 17:3 (above).

Did you notice the key phrase in Jesus's definition of eternal life? The key phrase is *to know You*. The phrase *to know* carries with it a huge meaning, which the *Amplified Bible* helps us understand more thoroughly. Reread the *Amplified Bible* version of John 17:3 (provided as starting Scripture for this week), and then read Philippians 3:10 (AMP) below; these passages describe eternal life and what it means "to know" God the Father and Son.

> *[For my determined purpose is] that I may know Him [that I may progressively become more deeply and intimately acquainted with Him, perceiving and recognizing and understanding the wonders of His Person more strongly and more clearly], and that I may in that same way come to know the power outflowing from His resurrection [which it exerts over believers], and that I may so share His sufferings as to be continually transformed [in spirit into His likeness even] to His death.*
>
> —PHILIPPIANS 3:10 (AMP)

Eternal life began the moment you came to know Jesus as your Savior. Time on earth should be seen as an opportunity to be increasingly more intimately acquainted with Him each day. Our life purpose is to become more and more thoroughly familiar with Him and His ways.

In order to know Him, you must have an intimate love relationship with God that is ever growing. Spending time with God each day and including Him in every detail of your life is crucial to this relationship. An unhurried time with God in the morning is the best way to begin to understand His plans and purposes for your day. Continually listening for His voice allows you to walk with God throughout the day.

Your love relationship will never become all that God intends unless you set aside time to grow, learn, and hear from Him. Ask God if your quiet time is a routine or a relationship. Ask Him to show you what He desires from your life, and be willing to adjust your schedule—and your life—to have an unhurried time with Him.

 Heavenly Father, may I come to know more of You today. Amen.

DIGGING DEEPER
THROUGH THE WEEK

How are you investing your time on earth? Are you setting goals to advance your career or to increase your fame? How much time are you investing in getting to know God intimately? What spiritual disciplines characterize your relationship with Him?

CALLED AND EQUIPPED

*Now to Him who is able to do exceedingly
abundantly above all that we ask or think,
according to the power that works in us, to Him
be glory in the church by Christ Jesus to all
generations, forever and ever. Amen.*

—EPHESIANS 3:20–21

Many times we have met people in various stages of life who say that they are just "ordinary people" with no special gifts or abilities. They usually say, "I don't know what God could use me to do." Have you ever excluded yourself from service to God because you did not feel qualified? The qualifications for being *called of God* are easily identifiable in 1 Corinthians 1:

> *For you see your calling, brethren, that not many wise according to the flesh, not many mighty, not many noble, are called. But God has chosen the foolish things of the world to put to shame the wise, and God has chosen the weak things of the world to put to shame the things which are mighty; and the base things of the world and the things which are despised God has chosen, and the things which are not, to bring to nothing the things that are, that no flesh should glory in His presence. But of Him you*

are in Christ Jesus, who became for us wisdom from God—and righteousness and sanctification and redemption—that, as it is written, "He who glories, let him glory in the LORD."

—1 CORINTHIANS 1:26–31

Based on this passage, do you think that God could and does desire to use your life in His kingdom? Yes! When God saved you, He had a plan to use your life.

God calls the weak, humble servant and shows Himself all-powerful through this person's life. It is this type of person God uses, because he or she is completely dependent on Him. When God does extraordinary things through an ordinary servant, the world sees indescribable activity that points to God. When they see God's indescribable activity, they are often drawn into a relationship with Him.

A common mistake we see is for Christians to assume that God won't use them but that He will use their pastor or church staff. At this point, we must emphasize that there is no separation or distinction in the call of God between Christian leaders and other Christians. All Christians are called to a saving faith, and in this call, all must release their lives to God for His purposes. God eternally planned that every believer would be spiritually equipped to both know and do the will of God, as He would reveal it to each one. And God promised that He would enable every believer to function this way by the empowering presence of His Holy Spirit. Therefore, each believer is called of God and is to function before God and a watching world as a priest unto God.

Too many times, we limit what God might want to do in us because of *self.* God chooses to use weak things to reveal Himself to the world. Don't let your opinion of yourself limit what God might want to do through you. Release your life to God, and let Him do more than you could ask or imagine through your life. This will show a watching world His power—bringing glory to Him.

 Father, today I release my life to You. Please use me to accomplish Your will this week in my family, my neighborhood, my workplace, and my church. Amen.

DIGGING DEEPER
THROUGH THE WEEK

Take time this week to read Exodus 35:30 through 36:1. Do you find it surprising that the Spirit equipped individuals to do all manner of work—building, wood carving, artistic works, tapestry making, and weaving? Often we assume the Spirit equips people to preach and teach the gospel. However, God equips His people in a wide range of talents to be used to bring honor to His name.

Ask God to show you how He has equipped you and how He desires to use your life.

Called to Lifelong Learning

*Then Jesus said to them, "Follow Me, and
I will make you become fishers of men."*

—Mark 1:17

Have you ever thought that you are not equipped to live out the call of God? Perhaps you don't have seminary training or maybe you weren't raised in a Christian home. Or has a past failure caused you to feel less than worthy to live out God's call with passion and purpose? In John 17, Jesus reveals a very important truth to us: He explains that the Father gives our lives to Jesus for Him to develop, teach, and equip us. For what purpose would that be? To make us vessels His Father can use to save a lost and dying world. In His significant prayer, Jesus said to the Father:

> *"I have glorified You on the earth. I have finished the work which You have given Me to do.... **I have manifested Your name to the men whom You have given Me out of the world. They were Yours, You gave them to Me, and they have kept Your word. Now they have known that all things which You have given Me are from You. For I have given to them the words which You have given Me; and they have received them,** and have known surely that I came forth from You; and they have*

> *believed that You sent Me.... And the glory which You gave Me*
> *I have given them, that they may be one just as We are one: I in*
> *them, and You in Me; that they may be made perfect in one,*
> *and that the world may know that You have sent Me, and have*
> *loved them as You have loved Me."*
>
> —JOHN 17:4, 6–8, 22–23
> (boldface added for emphasis)

When Jesus called the first disciples, He assured them of His responsibility for their lives: *"Follow Me, and I will make you become fishers of men"* (Mark 1:17). Whose responsibility was it for the disciples to become fishers of men? Jesus would be the One, who, under the instruction of the Father, would teach the disciples about the kingdom of God. They would, in turn, give their lives to following Jesus and become fishers of men. The disciples were simply responsible to stay with Jesus and to learn and practice what He taught.

You see, in order to live out God's call, we must be lifelong learners. In Matthew 11, Jesus invites us to learn of Him:

> *"Come to Me, all you who labor and are heavy laden, and I will*
> *give you rest. Take My yoke upon you and learn from Me, for*
> *I am gentle and lowly in heart, and you will find rest for your*
> *souls. For My yoke is easy and My burden is light."*
>
> —MATTHEW 11:28–30

Who is Jesus inviting into His restful presence? *All* we who labor and are heavy laden are invited to come to Him. Once we are in His presence, we are told to take His yoke and *learn* from Him. As we are yoked with Him, we will learn from Him and our character will become more and more like His.

All of the Gospels record how Jesus taught, trained, guided, encouraged, empowered, and fully equipped His disciples for all that the Father had in mind to do through them. Have you ever considered how Jesus has been equipping you for all that the heavenly Father has in mind for your life? Are you feeling weary with the weight of following Him? Release your life today—come to Jesus and let Him give you rest as He equips you!

Lord, I have been trying to serve You in my own strength. Please forgive me. Teach me, Lord, to bring my burdens to You and to take Your yoke and learn from You. Grant me a teachable spirit today and help me be a quick learner! Amen.

DIGGING DEEPER
THROUGH THE WEEK

When Jesus prayed the words of John 17, He was at the end of His earthly assignment. Take time this week to read John 17 several times. Consider your own life: Are you near the end of an assignment? Or perhaps you are near the end of your life on earth. In either case, can you stand before God and say, as Jesus did, *"I have finished the work which You have given Me to do"* (John 17:4)?

Accountable for Loyal Service

Also I heard the voice of the Lord, saying:
"Whom shall I send, and who will go for Us?"
Then I said, "Here am I! Send me."

—Isaiah 6:8

God is looking over our homes, churches, communities, and cities and beyond when He asks, *"Whom shall I send?"* *"Whom shall I send* into the schools or to the soccer and football fields?" *"Whom shall I send* into the community centers, the hospitals, and the business places?" We might look at Isaiah's response and think it is only for being sent to a great task. We might be listening for the booming voice of God calling out to see who will go forth to a worthwhile and visible ministry. But if we are not careful, we will miss the activity of God and His invitation for us to join Him in His present work while we wait for that "big" assignment.

How many children or young people make do without discipleship and how many people are missing out on hearing the gospel because no one responds to God's call to teach a Sunday School class or share their faith at work?

We need to be reminded of another Scripture:

"For the eyes of the LORD run to and fro throughout the whole earth, to show Himself strong on behalf of those whose heart is loyal to Him."

—2 CHRONICLES 16:9

According to this passage, what is God looking over the earth to do? Does it surprise you that God is looking for someone to use and work in to display His strength to a watching world? This verse should serve as encouragement to all Christians. God does not need our strength, our talents, or our plans; He simply wants our willing, obedient hearts. If we make our lives available to Him, He will, in turn, strengthen, empower, and equip us (show Himself strong in us) to accomplish His will so that the watching world will see His love.

What do you think the Lord sees when He looks at your life? Could He describe your heart as being loyal to Him? Do your actions reveal a heart that is loyal to Him? You can never fully estimate the value of your life to God. To God, eternity is always at stake! Your obedience releases the fullness of God in accomplishing His purpose through you.

Do you know of some areas in which He has been asking you to serve, but you have not yet responded? How is He sending you, as a child of God, to be involved in His work? Is your heart ready to respond to the Lord the way Isaiah did?

 Father, as I go about my busy day, please use me
to encourage someone who needs help today.
Send me, Lord! Amen.

DIGGING DEEPER
THROUGH THE WEEK

Let's consider an event in the life of Philip. God gave Philip a small, seemingly insignificant assignment: *"Arise and go toward the south along the road which goes down from Jerusalem to Gaza"* (Acts 8:26). Read about Philip's step-by-step obedience in loyal service to God as described in Acts 8:26–40, and answer the following questions:

1. What was the first part of Philip's assignment (v. 26)?

2. What was Philip's response (v. 27)?

3. When Philip stepped forward by faith and obeyed God's simple command, God then revealed the next step. What was the next step in Philip's assignment (v. 29)?

4. What was the end result of Philip's obedience (vv. 36–38)?

Philip obeyed God one step at a time. Through his obedience, the Ethiopian eunuch was saved. What seemed like an insignificant assignment, *"Arise and go toward the south,"* was God's plan to bring salvation to a man who could influence the queen he served and, thereby, potentially influence his entire country.

Never take lightly any assignment that God gives you. Always obey immediately.

CALLED TO CHARACTER
TRANSFORMATION

"But the Helper, the Holy Spirit, whom the
Father will send in My name, He will teach you
all things, and bring to your remembrance
all things that I said to you."

—JOHN 14:26

Too often Christians desire some evidence of Christian maturity or character without realizing it takes time—time with God. They want, for example, "the faith of Abraham," but they do not realize that it took God about 40 years to develop Abraham's character to the point where he would immediately respond to God's command to offer his only son, Isaac, as a sacrifice to God. God also brought Moses constantly before Him to remind him of his walk with God. He did this with David as well, and in Psalm 51, we see the major changes David had to make, the repentance and cleansing he needed to experience, to have *the joy of [God's] salvation"* restored in him (v. 12). Jesus had to take His disciples aside constantly to explain how their continuing lack of faith was affecting their relationship with Him.

God must take each of us aside regularly. He reminds us of His call in our lives, brings to our remembrance all He has said to us (see John 14:26), and helps us to see how we are responding to His shaping and guiding of our lives.

> *But we all, with unveiled face, beholding as in a mirror the glory of the Lord, are being transformed into the same image from glory to glory, just as by the Spirit of the Lord.*
>
> —2 CORINTHIANS 3:18

Paul assured believers that they could stand face-to-face with God, with no veil between them and God. But he said that when they stood face-to-face with God, they would be *"transformed into the same image from glory to glory"* (2 Corinthians 3:18). When a believer is face-to-face with God, an automatic "inventory" is taken by God to check out Christlikeness!

When we stand before God, we become very aware of our own lives. Do you remember Peter's response when he encountered Jesus in his fishing boat and acknowledged Him as Lord? Peter said, *"Depart from me, for I am a sinful man, O Lord!"* (Luke 5:8). Isaiah had a similar response when he met God in the Temple; he stated, *"Woe is me, for I am undone! Because I am a man of unclean lips, and I dwell in the midst of a people of unclean lips; for my eyes have seen the King, the LORD of hosts"* (Isaiah 6:5). Both of these men ultimately were used of God, but when they met the Lord, they saw themselves as God saw them, and they submitted their lives to God.

This standing before God comes when we, with transparent honesty, present ourselves for the *"washing of water by the word"* (Ephesians 5:26). The regular reading and study of God's Word is a must for all believers. The Holy Spirit will take the Word of God and apply it to our lives. When this happens, we need to recognize it as a face-to-face encounter with God!

Don't rush through these times of being before God; rather, wait for the Holy Spirit to do and say all that He wants you to understand. Meditate and pray over the words you are given. Prayer brings you into God's presence, where God changes your ways into His ways. Remain in the presence of God until you cry out as Jesus did, *"Not My will, but Yours, be done"* (Luke 22:42).

Heavenly Father, as I read Your words and pray throughout this week, open my understanding to Your will and Your plans. May Your perfect will be accomplished in my life. Amen.

DIGGING DEEPER
THROUGH THE WEEK

Set aside two hours this week to sit quietly before the Lord. Go to a place where you will be free from any distractions (that is, no cell phone, email, etc.). Have your Bible and your journal with you. Ask the Lord to show you what He thinks of your life and of your obedience to Him.

1. What is the Lord's response? What Scriptures does He lead you to read? What circumstance(s) does He bring to your remembrance? Write these things in your journal.

2. Do you need to make any adjustments as a result of this time spent with God?

CALLED TO TRUE FELLOWSHIP

"Not everyone who says to Me, 'Lord, Lord,'
shall enter the kingdom of heaven, but he who
does the will of My Father in heaven. Many
will say to Me in that day, 'Lord, Lord,
have we not prophesied in Your name, cast out
demons in Your name, and done many wonders
in Your name?' And then I will declare
to them, 'I never knew you; depart from Me,
you who practice lawlessness!'"

—MATTHEW 7:21–23

Our relationship with God is not based on our activities or our proclamation that we know Him. In Matthew 7:21–23, Jesus did not deny the wonders the people had done; He simply said He did not know them. They had never entered into a personal intimate fellowship with Him. He was not the Lord of their lives, regardless of their claims or activities.

Every person needs to settle this serious issue with God: Does the Lord know me? What is the evidence that I am in a vital, intimate fellowship with the Lord?

Many times in our ministry, God has revealed to us that individuals *can* be active in a church or involved in Christian activities without truly knowing Him. You see, we must each carefully examine our relationship with Jesus Christ and know that we *know* Him, and He us.

Jesus defined eternal life this way: *"And this is eternal life, that they may know You, the only true God, and Jesus Christ whom You have sent"* (John 17:3). To know Jesus Christ is *"to perceive, recognize, become acquainted with, and understand"* Him and His ways (see John 17:3 AMP). It is an ever-increasing and ongoing relationship of love with the person of Jesus Christ.

So crucial is this thorough knowledge of Jesus Christ to the purposes of God that the Father taught the disciples through Jesus how to have this relationship. It was almost three years into Jesus's ministry before Jesus finally asked them, *"Who do you say that I am?"* (Matthew 16:15). When Peter responded to Jesus, *"You are the Christ, the Son of the living God,"* Jesus assured him that he was right: *"Flesh and blood has not revealed this to you, but My Father who is in heaven."* Only then, with the disciples fully committed to who He was, was He able for the first time to introduce them to His cross and His coming death (see Matthew 16:16–17, 21).

Every believer must have a thorough, God-given, real, and personal relationship with Jesus Christ. The entire Christian life depends on it!

Dear Lord, this week I want to perceive, recognize,
become acquainted with, and understand You
more fully. Reveal Yourself to me as I serve You.
Lord, I want to know You more! Amen.

DIGGING DEEPER
THROUGH THE WEEK

Can your relationship with Christ be described as an ever-increasing and ongoing relationship of love with the person of Jesus Christ?

Take time this week to sit before the Lord and ask Him if He knows you. Ask Him to show you His perspective of your life—of your obedience and your service. Linger in the Word of God and in prayer to help you understand His viewpoint.

Maybe He is showing you that you must spend unhurried time with Him each day. If so, ask Him to show you what time He wants you to meet with Him each day so that your relationship with Him will become all that He desires. Once He shows you how to adjust your schedule, *obey!*

ACCOUNTABLE FOR MATURING SPIRITUALLY

For though by this time you ought to be teachers,
you need someone to teach you again the first
principles of the oracles of God; and you
have come to need milk and not solid food. For
everyone who partakes only of milk is unskilled
in the word of righteousness, for he is a babe.
But solid food belongs to those who are of full
age, that is, those who by reason of use have
their senses exercised to discern both
good and evil.

—HEBREWS 5:12–14

Often we may think we are mature in the faith simply because we have been Christians for many years. However, the Bible describes maturity by how we learn and understand the Word of God, implement the truths of God into our lives, and allow God to use us to teach others to grow in the faith.

It is important to note that the passage in Hebrews was an address to all the people and not simply the leaders. Each person was expected to grow and, in turn, teach others who were young in the faith. They should become teachers of the Word and, by skillful use of the Word, move from milk to meat. The church must help each believer to grow this way, to become mature and able to be of greater and greater use to God.

Maturity, however, takes time. It also requires obedience to Christ, who commanded believers not only to *"make disciples"* and baptize them, but also to teach them to observe all things He had commanded them (Matthew 28:19–20). This task is spiritually demanding but was faithfully practiced by early believers in Jerusalem, as seen in Acts 2:

> *Then those who gladly received his word were baptized; and that day about three thousand souls were added to them. And they continued steadfastly in the apostles' doctrine and fellowship, in the breaking of bread, and in prayers. Then fear came upon every soul, and many wonders and signs were done through the apostles. Now all who believed were together, and had all things in common, and sold their possessions and goods, and divided them among all, as anyone had need. So continuing daily with one accord in the temple, and breaking bread from house to house, they ate their food with gladness and simplicity of heart, praising God and having favor with all the people. And the Lord added to the church daily those who were being saved.*

> —ACTS 2:41–47

This is a simple, clear picture of a spiritual family, the local church, taking care of newborn believers. As we read the rest of the Book of Acts, we see how those believers soon were on mission with God all over their world. God really did accomplish His eternal purpose to redeem the lost through them. God has given us a clear picture of incredible fellowship and unprecedented spiritual growth among

His people. His desire is for every church to experience this same unity, fellowship, growth, and demonstration of His supernatural power in our day.

Lord, I pray that You would show me where
my life fits into Your plan for my church. Help me
to be growing more spiritually mature each day and
to encourage others in their growth. Amen.

DIGGING DEEPER
THROUGH THE WEEK

Read Ephesians 4, Romans 12, and 1 Corinthians 12 this week, and think about the following:

1. Is your church helping the members grow into maturity?

2. As you consider how God called and used those in the early church, ask God to show you where your life fits into His plan for your church.

God's desire is that once you have entered into a relationship with Him, you grow into maturity in the Christian life and, in turn, be used to help others grow in their faith. Has God strategically placed your life alongside someone who needs help growing to maturity in Christ? If so, don't waste a moment; ask God to guide you in helping those He has placed in your life for this purpose.

Called to Grow

*And the disciples came and said to Him,
"Why do You speak to them in parables?"
He answered and said to them, "Because it has
been given to you to know the mysteries of the
kingdom of heaven, but to them it has not been
given. For whoever has, to him more will be
given, and he will have abundance; but whoever
does not have, even what he has will be taken
away from him. Therefore I speak to them
in parables, because seeing they do not see,
and hearing they do not hear,
nor do they understand."*

—Matthew 13:10–13

As a child is fully equipped with physical senses to function in the physical world, so also is the Christian given spiritual senses to function in the spiritual world in his or her relationship with God. Spiritual senses help the Christian to hear God's voice and follow Him, to see His activity and join Him, and to have a heart that understands and obeys Him.

Read Matthew 13:10–13, and notice to whom the ability to understand the ways and thinking of the kingdom of heaven had been given. That ability had been given to the ones whom God had called, who, once called, chose to follow Christ—the disciples. Jesus clearly indicated to His disciples that since they had been called by God, they were different. For example, Jesus told them, *"It has been given to you to know the mysteries of the kingdom of heaven, but to them* [others who came to hear Jesus] *it has not been given"* (Matthew 13:11). This was followed by an astounding announcement from Jesus: *"But blessed are your eyes for they see, and your ears for they hear"* (Matthew 13:16).

As we grow in our relationship with Christ, we also develop "spiritual senses." Each believer must develop the use of his or her special spiritual senses. It is by the use of these senses that the believer grows. Each child of God must learn to hear and recognize the voice of God and to obey Him.

Jesus assures us that His followers, His sheep, are able to hear His voice, recognize it, and follow (obey) Him:

> *"But he who enters by the door is the shepherd of the sheep. To him the doorkeeper opens, and the sheep hear his voice; and he calls his own sheep by name and leads them out. And when he brings out his own sheep, he goes before them; and the sheep follow him, for they know his voice.... My sheep hear My voice, and I know them, and they follow Me."*
>
> —JOHN 10:2–4, 27

These principles must be firmly in place in the Christian's life for the fullness of God's calling to be experienced. Children of God are expected to go on to maturity. Part of this maturing is growing in the ability to hear, recognize, and see God and His activity.

As you mature in this relationship and develop your spiritual senses, you will come to hear, recognize, and understand the voice of God as He seeks to use your life for His purposes. Look back to this time last year. Can you see that your spiritual senses have become more keen?

 Heavenly Father, open my eyes to see Your activity.
Sharpen my spiritual senses so I don't miss anything
You are saying to me today. Amen.

DIGGING DEEPER
THROUGH THE WEEK

Take a moment to evaluate your spiritual senses:

1. Look back over the past month, and recall the things you have heard from the Lord.

2. What have you seen Him do in your life?

3. Ask Him to give you eyes to see His activity and ears to hear His commands and a willing, obedient heart to respond.

Perhaps you have heard Him say some things to which you haven't yet responded. Don't wait—respond obediently today! Partial obedience is disobedience!

WEEK 23

ACCOUNTABLE TO OBEY
AND HONOR GOD

*And whatever you do in word or deed, do all in the
name of the Lord Jesus, giving thanks to God
the Father through Him.*

—COLOSSIANS 3:17

Everything in the Christian's life rests on obedience! Obedience always unlocks the activity of God in a Christian's life. Obedience is the heart of experiencing a life on mission with God in the world.

It is encouraging to know that the Holy Spirit has been assigned to assist us in honoring God as we obey God and His call on our lives. Often we can get discouraged or afraid when we see the assignments ahead of us. However, it is important to realize that we are only instructed to follow one step at a time and be concerned with one day at a time. Remember that Jesus has warned us not to worry about tomorrow (Matthew 6:34), but to simply turn each day over to the Lord and release our lives to obey whatever He commands.

As believers, we should live each day with the understanding that we are accountable to God for every word we say and every thought we think. We should always be listening for the

Lord to say, *"Well done,"* as we live out our Christianity before a watching world.

A time of accountability with God will come. Jesus clearly indicated this to His disciples; Matthew 25 has several examples. It will be a serious time before God, and He will reward everyone according to his or her faithful obedience to the Master.

As you read the following passages, notice Paul's sense of accountability and urgency to honor God in the call He had placed on his life.

> *But by the grace of God I am what I am, and His grace toward me was not in vain; but I labored more abundantly than they all, yet not I, but the grace of God which was with me.*
>
> —1 Corinthians 15:10

> *And whatever you do, do it heartily, as to the Lord and not to men, knowing that from the Lord you will receive the reward of the inheritance; for you serve the Lord Christ.*
>
> —Colossians 3:23–24

To live without a real sense of accountability is to lose a major motivation in serving our Lord! Just to know that not a thing we do goes without His notice and love brings comfort. To love Him with all our heart, soul, mind, and strength brings with it such an intimate relationship and spontaneous, joyful accountability. All those who have been greatly used of God lived this way.

Obedience is a by-product of our accountability to God. As we grow in our accountability to the Lord, we will unhesitatingly and immediately obey Him. Note what Jesus says about obedience:

"If anyone loves me, he will obey my teaching. My Father will love him, and we will come to him and make our home with him. He who does not love me will not obey my teaching."

—JOHN 14:23–24 (NIV)

 Heavenly Father, may I live my life today "as to the Lord and not to men," and may I do it with a deeply grateful heart to You. Amen.

DIGGING DEEPER
THROUGH THE WEEK

Evaluate your obedience to God and to what He has shown you:

1. Is your obedience to God unlocking the activity of God in and through your life? What are some examples?

2. Are there areas of your life that you have not fully surrendered to God—areas in which you have not obeyed Him?

Spend some time before the Lord, and ask Him if you have been faithful to obey *all* He has been asking you to do. Write down what God tells you about your obedience to Him and His claim on your life. How have you honored Him?

CALLED TO JOIN GOD'S WORK

*But Jesus answered them, "My Father
has been working until now, and I have been
working."... "Most assuredly, I say to you,
the Son can do nothing of Himself, but what
He sees the Father do; for whatever He does,
the Son also does in like manner. For the Father
loves the Son, and shows Him all things that
He Himself does; and He will show Him
greater works than these, that you may marvel."*

—JOHN 5:17, 19–20

Jesus said that the Father is at work in the world. Jesus, being His chosen servant, said the Son (Servant) does not take the initiative, but rather watches to see where the Father (Master) is working and joins Him. Because the Father loves the Son, He shows Him everything that He Himself is doing. The Son joins in with the Father, working together with Him. It is then that the Father is able to complete all He has purposed to do through the Son. God purposed to bring a lost world back to Himself, and He does it through His Son, who loves, trusts, and obeys the Father.

This same pattern is true for how the Father involves us in His work today. Because we are Christians and because of the

80

relationship of love between the Father and Christians, He shows us where He is working. When He shows us His work, we must be quick to join Him and, in turn, become workers together with Christ.

Amos, the prophet, was a layman (a shepherd and a caretaker of sycamore-fig trees). He described his life this way:

> *"I was no prophet, nor was I a son of a prophet, but I was a sheepbreeder and a tender of sycamore fruit. Then the* LORD *took me as I followed the flock, and the* LORD *said to me, 'Go, prophesy to My people Israel.'"*
>
> —AMOS 7:14–15

God had an urgent message that His people, Israel, needed to hear immediately! Time was running out for them. Judgment was very near. God wanted them to hear from Him about His love one more time. Amos was the man God chose to take His message to His people. It surprised Amos, but he responded obediently, and God accomplished His purposes through him. Though God's people did not heed His message, they knew God had spoken to them through Amos.

As God has worked and moved throughout history to accomplish His eternal purpose, so He does today. Always, eternity is in the balance. Those He chooses, calls, shapes, and uses are deeply and often painfully aware of His assignment. They are the clay and God is the potter. God always has a design in mind when He chooses a person and invites that person to join Him in His work. This God-chosen process is the way God calls you and works through your life too.

Have you ever felt like Amos when he said, *"I was no prophet, nor was I a son of a prophet"*? Often we quote the first part of Amos's words but do not follow through with the obedience of Amos. If God has called you, obey immediately! The safest place you and your family can be is in the place of obedience, as you seek to fully follow God's plan as shown through His Word.

Dear Lord, I know You are working to redeem a lost and dying world. I want to join You today in this work. Please use me today in any way You choose. May my heart be ready to obey the moment You direct me. Amen.

Digging Deeper
THROUGH THE WEEK

Has God called you to an assignment in which you have felt inadequate to serve? Have you made excuses that have kept you from obeying? If so, settle this with God today. Don't let another moment pass until you have thoroughly set your heart to obey *everything* He has commanded you to do and say.

Called and Set Apart

Then the word of the LORD came to me, saying:
"Before I formed you in the womb I knew you;
before you were born I sanctified you;
I ordained you a prophet to the nations."

—JEREMIAH 1:4–5

When God wanted to speak clearly and forcefully to His people, Judah, He chose Jeremiah to be His spokesperson. But the heart of God knew before Jeremiah was even born that He had set him apart for this important time in history. This time was critical for His people. God wanted both a long and a passionate pleading from His heart to come to His people. Jeremiah was then shaped by God to be the one through whom He would speak. So tender was the message to Judah that Jeremiah was called the weeping prophet! Listen to what happened:

Then the word of the LORD came to me, saying: "Before I formed
you in the womb I knew you; before you were born I sanctified
you; I ordained you a prophet to the nations." Then said I: "Ah,
Lord GOD! Behold, I cannot speak, for I am a youth." But the
LORD said to me: "Do not say, 'I am a youth,' for you shall
go to all to whom I send you, and whatever I command you,

you shall speak. Do not be afraid of their faces, for I am with you to deliver you," says the LORD. Then the LORD put forth His hand and touched my mouth, and the LORD said to me: "Behold, I have put My words in your mouth. See, I have this day set you over the nations and over the kingdoms, to root out and to pull down, to destroy and to throw down, to build and to plant."

—JEREMIAH 1:4–10

Have you ever felt like Jeremiah and stated, "I am only a youth and cannot speak or stand before the people"? God is not looking for all of your qualifications, talents, and abilities; He is looking for your submission to His call. He will give you the words, the opportunities, and the ability. He wants you to give Him your heart—that is, your trust, faith, and willingness to serve.

In every generation, God has shaped messengers through whom He could speak and work. As we walk with the Lord, we must not forget that God will be shaping and molding us for His purposes for our generation. When God puts a deep accountability on our hearts to serve Him, we must make sure we recognize God's shaping hand on our lives and His current desire to use our lives. God wants only our hearts and availability to Him. He can and will shape us for the assignment, but He needs for us to step out and allow Him access to fashion our lives for use in His eternal plan.

Those God chooses and calls know it is God, know what He is saying, and know how they are to release their lives to Him for His purposes in their day!

Heavenly Father, I don't know or understand why
You would call me for a task like the one that is before
 me. Please forgive me for not trusting You with my
life and with the lives of my family members. I release
my life to You. Please guide me now in Your truth.
In Jesus's name, Amen.

DIGGING DEEPER
THROUGH THE WEEK

Before Samuel was born, his life was set apart for service to God (1 Samuel 1:11). He was the only person in the history of God's people to serve as a prophet, a priest, and a judge. Samuel was also an intercessor (1 Samuel 7:8–13).

Read 1 Samuel 1:8–28; 2:18–21; and 3:7.

God's purpose for Samuel's life was enormous! The same is true for your life. Has God called you to an assignment in which you have felt inadequate to serve? Have you made excuses that have kept you from obeying? Stop. Take time to pray and spend unhurried time before the Lord. Don't take another step until you have spent time before God concerning this assignment.

Accountable for Daily Obedience

"He has filled him with the Spirit of God, in wisdom and understanding, in knowledge and all manner of workmanship."

—Exodus 35:31

Moses's daily walk with God, guiding God's people, was exceedingly demanding for him. It required the full presence and enabling that only the Spirit of God could bring. But God also provided 70 other key leaders to share this leadership load. In their new assignment, they would require the enabling from the same Spirit of God. This enabling provided thoroughly and adequately all that was needed for the leaders to guide God's people according to His commands and purposes.

After some of Moses's leadership responsibilities had been delegated, God commanded Moses to build a tabernacle for His presence among His people. It would require the utmost care and obedience to all God would direct. God told Moses He had already chosen and placed His Spirit on some men who would do all that He commanded (see Exodus 35:30 through 36:1). They were ordinary workmen, chosen by God and equipped by God's Spirit to do His will in all things.

Do you find it surprising that the Spirit equipped them to do building, wood carving, artistic works, tapestry making, and weaving? Often we assume that the Spirit equips people only to preach or teach the gospel. However, God equips His people in a wide range of talents to be used to bring honor to His name.

This pattern of God working through ordinary people, called, assigned, and enabled by God, continued through each of the judges of Israel. Each was called at a crucial moment in the life of God's people—a time when they needed deliverance from their enemies. David's life followed this same pattern (1 Samuel 16:13); the disciples and the Apostle Paul were also shaped and used by God in their day.

Now it is our turn. This is especially true because God has huge purposes to accomplish through His people in our generation. So much is in the balance, especially eternally. The heart of God has not changed. He is *not willing that any should perish but that all should come to repentance"* (2 Peter 3:9). So in this our day and in our lives, the following is still incredibly true:

> *For the eyes of the LORD run to and fro throughout the whole earth, to show Himself strong on behalf of those whose heart is loyal to Him.*
>
> —2 CHRONICLES 16:9

The key to being used by God is the condition of our hearts and our willingness to respond in obedience to His call on our lives. Our usefulness to God does not lie in our abilities or talents or in the lack of them, but in our willingness to be used by God to accomplish His desires. So the process continues. But now it involves you, and it involves me! And God is watching to see how we will respond to Him.

Dear Lord, I feel so very ordinary, and I cannot imagine how my life could be useful to You—the Creator of the universe. But I know that You have called me and desire to use me in Your plans for this generation. All I can say is, "Here am I, Lord; send me." In the name of Jesus, Amen.

DIGGING DEEPER
THROUGH THE WEEK

Jesus reminds us, *"Without Me you can do nothing"* (John 15:5). Here is another way of saying this: "Without the enabling presence of the Holy Spirit guiding your life, you can do absolutely nothing of eternal value."

Look back over the past few days. Did the presence of the Holy Spirit enable you to "do all things"—to act in ways that please God and have eternal value? What about your personal relationships: Did you allow the Holy Spirit to guide you as you related to people? Specifically consider how you related to the following people:

- Marriage partner

- Children

- Co-workers

- Boss/employer

- Pastor/staff

- Neighbor

Called to the Learning Process

"Come to Me, all you who labor and are heavy-laden and overburdened, and I will cause you to rest. [I will ease and relieve and refresh your souls.] Take My yoke upon you and learn of Me, for I am gentle (meek) and humble (lowly) in heart, and you will find rest (relief and ease and refreshment and recreation and blessed quiet) for your souls."

—Matthew 11:28–29 (AMP)

If you are in a situation in which you feel overwhelmed and inundated with the concerns of your life, let us encourage you to quickly *come to Jesus!* Because when God calls us, He thoroughly and completely equips us, enabling us to respond obediently to Him in every matter of life and to walk peacefully through any situation.

In order to be equipped, we must remain in the hands of the Equipper! God is on mission, and the servant of the Lord must be where the Master is. Jesus said, *"If anyone serves Me, let him follow Me; and where I am, there My servant will be also"* (John 12:26a). And Jesus added, significantly, *"If anyone serves Me, him My Father will honor"* (v. 26b). Whole books could be written on this intimate relationship between the Lord and His servants. This closeness, this proximity with the Master, is needed for the called to receive the provision.

The enabling provision of God for His servants is clearly declared and seen throughout Scripture and history. Some of the provisions of God are clear. For example, we know Paul's words in Philippians 4:19: *"And my God will meet all your needs according to his glorious riches in Christ Jesus"* (NIV). Did you notice how many of your needs God promises to meet? In 2 Corinthians 1:20, Paul reminds us that *"all the promises of God in Him [Jesus Christ] are Yes, and in Him Amen, to the glory of God through us."* And in 2 Peter, we see this encouraging message:

> *His divine power has given to us all things that pertain to life and godliness, through the knowledge of Him who called us by glory and virtue, by which have been given to us exceedingly great and precious promises, that through these you may be partakers of the divine nature, having escaped the corruption that is in the world through lust.*

> —2 PETER 1:3–4

If we were to take each phrase of these verses to heart, our lives would have absolutely no room for worrying or fretting, no room for complaining or for feeling inadequate in our Christian life, no room for laziness or depression. God's provisions are perfect and always on time for His children.

What are you facing this week? Is it an impossible situation with no hope of a positive outcome? Let us remind you of one final verse: *"For with God nothing is ever impossible and no word from God shall be without power or impossible of fulfillment"* (Luke 1:37 AMP).

*Almighty God, You are my God, and I know
that Your power is perfect to meet any need I have.
Help me, Lord, to take Your yoke on my shoulders
and carefully learn from You this week. Amen.*

DIGGING DEEPER
THROUGH THE WEEK

First Peter 5:7 provides instructions as to what to do about worries and anxiety: Cast *"the whole of your care [all your anxieties, all your worries, all your concerns, once and for all] on Him, for He cares for you affectionately and cares about you watchfully"* (AMP). The only cure for worry or anxiety is to come to Jesus (Matthew 11:28–29) and to leave your cares with Him.

Anxiety and faith are opposites—you cannot walk in faith and, at the same time, be filled with worry. As soon as anxiety comes into your life, faith is squashed. Faith in God will never disappoint; it will always dissolve worry.

Take time this week to cast all your cares upon the Lord. Leave them there, and walk in the freedom of faith in your heavenly Father.

CALLED TO COMPLETENESS

"However, when He, the Spirit of truth,
has come, He will guide you into all truth;
for He will not speak on His own authority,
but whatever He hears He will speak; and
He will tell you things to come."

—JOHN 16:13

The greatest of God's provisions is His Holy Spirit. Jesus assured His disciples, *"You shall receive power when the Holy Spirit has come upon you"* (Acts 1:8). He had earlier told them, *"I will pray the Father, and He will give you another Helper, that He may abide with you forever—the Spirit of truth"* (John 14:16–17). He (the Holy Spirit) would always let the believers know the Father's will for each of them (John 16:13; 1 Corinthians 2:9–16). He would guide them into all truth, teach them all things, and bring to their remembrance everything Christ had commanded them (John 16:13–15; John 14:26). He would also help them when they prayed (Romans 8:26), an activity that would be so much a part of their relationship with God and the fulfillment of His will in their lives. And the Holy Spirit would work the Scriptures into their lives to serve as a "sword" (Ephesians 6:17).

All that was available to people in the Scriptures is available today to every believer called of God.

The Holy Spirit is God Himself, present and active, enabling every believer to do whatever God commands. No matter what it is that God commands the believer to do with Him, His provision is already present and available, and the Holy Spirit is actively working to implement all of it into that believer's life. No matter how difficult or impossible an assignment God places on the life of one of His children, God's provision will completely enable that person to do it.

God's provision for every believer on mission with Him is the fullness of His presence. In His presence, each believer is *"complete."* Paul describes it this way: *"For in Him dwells all the fullness of the Godhead bodily; and you are complete in Him, who is the head of all principality and power"* (Colossians 2:9–10). Every believer is enabled to experience God's finishing work, as Paul states in Philippians: *"being confident of this very thing, that He who has begun a good work in you will complete it until the day of Jesus Christ"* (Philippians 1:6).

The Holy Spirit does this completing or enabling in many ways. One way of enabling comes as the believer spends time in God's Word. In the midst of the study, the Holy Spirit gives a confirming *yes* to what He knows to be the will of God. It comes as a quiet assurance, giving peace and joy. He also gives affirmation when the believer takes time to pray and seek assurance from God of His will. To the carefully observant person who prays, there comes a quiet direction to the prayer, putting the person into the center of the will of God (Romans 8:26–28). When John was praying on the island of Patmos, the Holy Spirit gave him clear direction concerning the will of God (Revelation 1).

Holy Spirit, You are alive in my heart and speak to
me each day. Thank You for bringing to my memory
all of the commands of God; thank You for convicting
me of sin; thank You for enabling me to live out all
that God requires of me. Amen.

Digging Deeper
THROUGH THE WEEK

What affirmations and enabling has God brought to your life from prayer and Bible study this past month? Take a moment to read through your spiritual journal from the past few weeks, and let the Holy Spirit remind you of the words He spoke to you and the things He has revealed to you about your life and service.

Called Together

For as the body is one and has many members,
but all the members of that one body, being many,
are one body, so also is Christ.

—1 Corinthians 12:12

Christians will know more completely when they are being called by God as they function in the life of His church (the body of Christ). The most complete pictures of the body working together are found in 1 Corinthians 12, Ephesians 4, and Romans 12. Each member in the body functions where God places him or her in the body, and each assists the other parts of the body to grow up into the Head, which is Christ. This is not merely a figure of speech; it is a living reality. The loving Christ is truly present in the church body, and each member really does assist the others in knowing and doing the will of God.

Paul constantly affirmed his need of other believers to help him know and carry out the call of God in his life.

> *For I long to see you, that I may impart to you some spiritual gift,*
> *so that you may be established—that is, that I may be encouraged*
> *together with you by the mutual faith both of you and me.*
>
> —Romans 1:11–12

And [pray] for me, that utterance may be given to me, that I may open my mouth boldly to make known the mystery of the gospel, for which I am an ambassador in chains; that in it I may speak boldly, as I ought to speak.

—EPHESIANS 6:19–20

How is your life currently encouraging others in their faith in the church you attend? Are you allowing others in your church to encourage you? In the church where God has placed you, He has provided other believers whom He has equipped to assist you in knowing God's call and activity in your life and whom He has chosen to assist you in carrying out His will.

Your involvement, or activity, in the body of Christ is crucial if God is to carry out His eternal purpose for your life today. The eye can help the ear to know what it is hearing, the hand to know what it is feeling, and the feet to know where to step next. The life of the body is affected by each member relating in love to one another (Ephesians 4:16).

Understanding this will involve you not only in your church family but also with other churches (as happened in the New Testament) in your local area, across the nation, and around the world. God's call is to take the gospel to every person and into every nation. God's plan for accomplishing this is to call you to Himself and then place your life alongside all the others He has called, so that He can work dramatically across an entire world through His people, working together as one—you being a part of the whole!

God's call in your life always includes your intimate involvement with His people in and through your local church.

*Dear Lord, help me to faithfully live out the call
in the middle of the church in which You have
placed me. Amen.*

DIGGING DEEPER
THROUGH THE WEEK

Read 1 Corinthians 12 through 13 several times this week. As you read Paul's vivid description of the *"body of Christ"* in chapter 12, recognize that all spiritual gifts are the manifestation of the indwelling Spirit of God (1 Corinthians 12:4–7). The purpose of the gifts is for the building up of the body of Christ—the church.

Prayerfully consider where God has placed you and your family and how the Holy Spirit is working through you to build up the body of Christ. Don't overlook the message Paul gives in 1 Corinthians 13. Both chapters are absolutely vital. Love is the greatest gift and must be expressed in each believer's life within the church.

Called and Affirmed

Let your conduct be without covetousness;
be content with such things as you have.
For He Himself has said, "I will never
leave you nor forsake you."

—Hebrews 13:5

The heart that seeks God finds Him; the person who asks Him receives; to the one who knocks, God opens a door (Matthew 7:7–11). God responds to His children, and they know that it is God who is affirming their relationship with Him. It is a living, ongoing relationship of love!

When you are in a personal relationship with God, He, in love, affirms His presence and His call in your life daily! This is not simply a feeling, but is a conviction of His eternal faithfulness.

As you, an earnest seeker, open the Scriptures, the Holy Spirit is present and actively seeking to bring you into the will of God. Words suddenly have new meanings and seem to apply directly to your life—and they really do. This is the affirmation of God in your life through the working of the Holy Spirit. The same is true of all Scripture—in particular, the life and teachings of Jesus: *"All Scripture is given by inspiration of God, and is profitable for doctrine, for reproof, for correction, for instruction in righteousness"* (2 Timothy 3:16).

Throughout the entire process, the Holy Spirit *"bears witness with [your] spirit"* not only that you are a child of God but also that you are in the center of the will of God (Romans 8:16, 27).

Sometimes God uses friends or family or persons in your church to give you affirmation for your call. Someone shares a Scripture with you that is the very same Scripture God gave you that morning. This is God's affirmation! A timely phone call or email comes. Again, it's God's affirmation to your life and call. A caution or even a word of correction becomes God's affirmation not to proceed. Remember that you do not live your Christian life in isolation. You live out God's call upon your life alongside the rest of God's people.

Additional cautions need to be shared at this point. If you see no affirming presence of God in your life or ministry, you need to stop and see if, indeed, you may be out of God's will, and He is speaking to you by *not* giving affirmation to your sin, rebellion, and disobedience. It is also important to remember that *success* as the world defines it may not at all be the affirming presence of God. God never leaves His children to guess whether they are walking in the center of His will. He provides plenty of daily assurances. Remember, there are no coincidences in the life wholly yielded to God! God is completely involved in the life of the one He calls to go with Him.

 Father, I thank You that You never leave me or forsake me—that You are ever present in my life. You are so good! Amen.

DIGGING DEEPER
THROUGH THE WEEK

The heart that is earnestly seeking God will daily spend time in His Word. When you do this, the Holy Spirit uses the Word of God like a sword (Ephesians 6:17) to convict you of sin, to *"guide you into all truth,"* to *"teach you all things,"* to *"bring to your remembrance"* all that Christ has been saying to you, and to help you thoroughly understand and apply His will and call to your life (John 14:26; 16:7–15).

Take time this week to meditate on the things the Father has been teaching you recently. The following questions will help guide you through this process:

1. Has the Word of God brought conviction of sin to your heart?

2. Has God used His Word to *"guide you into all truth"*?

3. Is the Holy Spirit teaching you *"all things"* as you study the Bible?

4. Did the Holy Spirit *"bring to your remembrance"* all that Christ has said to you in the past months?

5. Are you able to understand and apply God's will and call to your life?

6. How has God affirmed His activity in your life this week?

Called to Pray

Rejoice always, pray without ceasing,
in everything give thanks; for this is the will
of God in Christ Jesus for you.

—1 Thessalonians 5:16–18

Being called of God, you should expect to be shaped by Him in every area of your life. Expect God to change your regular quiet time into a thriving and intimate encounter with the Creator of the universe. Expect Scripture to leap off the page and for God to apply the words to the current events in your life. Expect God to radically change your prayer life, for it is in your prayer life that He will shape your character into the likeness of His Son.

Many of the most cherished times you will have with God will come in the middle of prayer. How much time are you spending in prayer each day? How much time should you spend in prayer each day? Only God can answer this question, as it is based on His agenda for the day.

Let's consider another question: Is it more important to speak or to listen when you pray? Prayer is the opportunity for God to speak to you and to transform your heart, mind, and will to be in harmony with His. In order to be a good pray-er, you must be a good listener!

If you have a heart that seeks after God, you will want to spend much time in prayer. God has given the Holy Spirit the responsibility to guide you into the will of God as you pray (Romans 8:26–27). Too often, prayers start off quite self-centered and self-focused. If you notice this happening, just continue to pray. Soon your prayer will change in focus and become God-centered; this is the Holy Spirit at work, according to the will of God. Follow the Spirit's directives immediately and completely.

Have you ever started to pray and realized your heart was filled with anger, even resentment, against someone or some situation? If this happens, recognize it as sin and repent. Soon after, God's love will fill your heart, and your prayer will change to expressions of love and blessing. This is God. By filling you with love, God affirms not only His presence but also His will for your life.

As God lays His heart over yours in prayer, it always creates an attitude of thanksgiving. Don't rush out of prayer without taking time to thank God for giving you His perspective. Always thank Him and alter everything to follow His directives, for He is ready to bless you greatly!

 Heavenly Father, what a privilege it is to pray to You and to have fellowship with You throughout the day. Please lay Your heart for this day over mine, and help me to see every circumstance through Your eyes. Amen.

DIGGING DEEPER
THROUGH THE WEEK

One of the most demanding assignments in the kingdom of God is intercessory prayer. Praying like Jesus means staying before the

Father in prayer until you have His perspective. Spend time this week in prayer—quiet, intentional, uninterrupted prayer.

Let Jesus's prayer life be your example and serve as a pattern for your own prayer life. Take time this week to meditate on the following passages that describe Jesus's prayer life:

1. Matthew 14:23

2. Mark 1:35

3. Luke 3:21–22

4. Luke 5:16

5. Luke 6:12

6. Luke 11:1

7. Luke 22:44

8. Luke 23:34, 46

9. Hebrews 5:7–9

ACCOUNTABLE FOR AWARENESS

*Then Jesus answered and said to them,
"Most assuredly, I say to you, the Son can do
nothing of Himself, but what He sees the Father
do; for whatever He does, the Son also does in like
manner. For the Father loves the Son, and shows
Him all things that He Himself does; and He
will show Him greater works than these, that you
may marvel. For as the Father raises the dead and
gives life to them, even so the Son gives life
to whom He will."*

—JOHN 5:19–21

God's provisions for a relationship with Him are completely thorough. Nothing is missing from God's perspective. God doesn't want us to miss His calling. All through the Scriptures, we see God speaking to His people and their responses of obedience or disobedience. What would it take to miss His calling? We would have to resist, quench, and grieve Him, His Son, and His Holy Spirit to miss His call.

When you are a Christian living in the world, God is actively at work in your life the moment you begin to sense an inner desire to do the will of God. God's timing for your full response is in place! This is the activity of God in your life causing you to want to do His will. The activity of God may be experienced while you are studying the Bible, when you are worshipping in your church, when you are praying, in the midst of your daily routine, or even when you are talking with a friend or one of your family members. Some things only God can do. Creating awareness of His call is something only God can do in a believer's life.

God Himself places within the heart of every believer the deepest desire to experience the strong presence and power of God working in and through that believer. God will not override a believer's heart or will, but He will thoroughly influence that life toward His will and His call. Notice this Scripture passage:

> *Therefore, my beloved, as you have always obeyed, not as in my presence only, but now much more in my absence, work out your own salvation with fear and trembling; for it is God who works in you both to will and to do for His good pleasure.*
>
> —PHILIPPIANS 2:12–13

But how, from the scriptural revelation, do you come to experience in life the deep reality of being called and accountable?

As you look for the answer to this question, it is important to remember that not only does God work in you *"both to will and to do for His good pleasure,"* but also *"He who has begun a good work in you will complete it until the day of Jesus Christ"* (Philippians 1:6). This is a wonderful verse to encourage you to never quit or give up, because God is always faithful to finish the work and complete all He desires to do through your life if you will let Him.

Dear Lord, I know You are working in the world today. Please show me where You are working in my world, and let me join You. Amen.

DIGGING DEEPER
THROUGH THE WEEK

If you ever wanted to pray earnestly for someone, praying directly from Ephesians 3:14–21 would be a good place to start. Read this passage right now and then answer the following questions:

1. What does Paul ask God to grant to the Ephesian church?

   • Verse 16

   • Verse 17

   • Verse 18

   • Verse 19

2. According to verse 20, what is God able to give or to do?

3. When God fulfills the things listed in verses 16–20, where does He receive the glory (v. 21)?

Accountable for Unity

*I therefore, a prisoner for the Lord, urge you
to walk in a manner worthy of the calling to which
you have been called, with all humility and
gentleness, with patience, bearing with one another
in love, eager to maintain the unity of the Spirit
in the bond of peace.*

—Ephesians 4:1–3 (ESV)

Living out the call of God will involve those around you in your local church. This truth is clearly seen throughout Scripture; for example, Matthew 18:19–20 states: *"Again I say to you that if two of you agree on earth concerning anything that they ask, it will be done for them by My Father in heaven. For where two or three are gathered together in My name, I am there in the midst of them."* God promises that He will be *"in the midst of"* those who are gathered together in agreement in His name.

Seeking to be in harmony is foundational as you live out your life in the body of Christ. But what should you do if, in the midst of following God, a conflict arises? Or what if someone lies about you or misunderstands your words? What if a difference in theology causes conflict in your church body? What are you to do?

First, you must get God's perspective. God's Word is filled with instructions related to conflict among believers. For example, in Romans, Paul instructs Christians to live in harmony and humility: *"Live in harmony with one another; do not be haughty (snobbish, high-minded, exclusive), but readily adjust yourself to [people, things] and give yourselves to humble tasks. Never overestimate yourself or be wise in your own conceits"* (Romans 12:16 AMP). (See also 1 Corinthians 1:10 and 1 Peter 3:8–9.) Harmony can be achieved only when all who are involved *"readily adjust"* themselves to one another and *"give [themselves] to humble tasks."* You must walk in humility, gentleness, and patience within the body of Christ. Walking in humility before God will enable you to walk in humility with others.

In John 13:20, Jesus says, *"Most assuredly, I say to you, he who receives whomever I send receives Me; and he who receives Me receives Him who sent Me."* Are you *"receiving"* those within your church family in the same way you would receive Jesus? Are you talking to them and treating them in the same way you would treat the Lord?

The Scriptures are clear with regard to how Christians are to relate to each other as they serve God together. The key to walking in harmony with other believers is to be humble and kind, keeping your integrity before God at all costs. Disunity among God's people is costly in the kingdom and in eternity. Fights and quarrels are self-centered—never God-centered. Don't allow yourself to partake in gossip or fighting; rather, be a part of the solution through intercessory prayer, through Bible study, and by being filled with the Spirit.

One of the greatest deterrents to living out the call of God is to become entangled in conflict among God's people. Every Christian will encounter potentially difficult situations and people. Remember to walk with all humility, gentleness, and patience so that you do not get sidetracked from God's call.

*Heavenly Father, I pray for my family and
my church to be perfectly united with You and always
to express love and kindness to each other. May I be
ready to adjust in order to bring or keep unity in
my family and my church. Help me be humble
and kind today. Amen.*

DIGGING DEEPER
THROUGH THE WEEK

Can you sincerely say that your life can be described like the passages
mentioned in this devotional (Romans 12:16; 1 Corinthians 1:10;
1 Peter 3:8–9)? Are you facing any conflicts this week? If you are
facing a conflict, ask God to help you walk in harmony with others.
Be very honest, and hold yourself accountable to God's standard for
a Christian facing conflict.

ACCOUNTABLE TO BE A WITNESS

*We give thanks to the God and Father of
our Lord Jesus Christ, praying always for you,
since we heard of your faith in Christ Jesus
and of your love for all the saints.*

—COLOSSIANS 1:3–4

When you recognize God's call on your life, it is important to bear witness to the call of God and to testify of how He is causing you to live out this call. When you bear witness to the call of God and then live out the call among God's people, it will serve as an encouragement to others to step out in faith and service to God.

The Book of Philemon is Paul's shortest letter recorded in Scripture. He wrote it to Philemon to let him know that Onesimus (Philemon's runaway slave) had become a true follower of Jesus Christ. However, before addressing the issue of Onesimus in this letter, Paul greeted his beloved friend and acknowledged Philemon's life of service: *"For we have great joy and consolation in your love, because the hearts of the saints have been refreshed by you, brother"* (Philemon 7). Philemon is described as one who refreshes the hearts of the saints. How would your fellow church members describe your life as you live out the call of God on your life? Would they say, "That person's life always refreshes and brings joy to my life"? How would you describe your fellow church members or your church staff? Do you describe them with fond affection and kind, loving words?

When Paul heard of the testimony of the Colossian church, he gave *"thanks to the God and Father of our Lord Jesus Christ"* (Colossians 1:3). What do other churches in your community do when they hear your church's name? Have you ever considered how the community around your church views the Christians within your church? Do they want to know the God you serve because of the reputation of your church and its people?

Many times people around you have a desire to follow God but are afraid to step out in faith. As you follow God, share how God is working in your life. Your personal testimony will serve as a source of encouragement to other individuals who may be hesitant to release their own life to God. People around you may be looking for an example of how God faithfully "walks" with a person striving to honor God. Further, sharing your calling with your church (or small group, Sunday School class, or discipleship class) and living out this call within the fellowship of the church will serve as an encouragement to the entire church body. Letting your church hear how God is at work in and through your life will keep the activity of God before the people and serve as a source of joy to your church leadership.

Dear Lord, may I live my life today recognizing that
I represent You. Let my words and actions be pleasing
to You at all times and in all circumstances. Cause my
testimony of Your activity to be a source
of encouragement to others. Amen.

Digging Deeper
THROUGH THE WEEK

Throughout Paul's letters, he continually explained the way in which he was living out the call of God. He was careful to share his testimony and describe his calling with the early church. This served to encourage them, to set an example for them, and to stir them to follow the call of God in their own lives. Read the following passages in which Paul described his understanding of his life and ministry:

1. Philippians 1:12–18

2. 1 Thessalonians 2:1–12

3. 1 Timothy 1:12–17

How would others describe your life and service to God? How would you describe your life and service to God? Take time this week to write down key events that make up your testimony, and be ready to share when God gives you an opportunity.

WEEK 35

CALLED FOR GOD'S AGENDA

Now in the morning, having risen a long while
before daylight, He went out and departed
to a solitary place; and there He prayed.

—MARK 1:35

Living out the call of God in your life begins with and is sustained through your daily relationship with God. In your quiet time—when you are alone with God—God speaks to you and guides you to know and understand His agenda. In the morning—and any other time He chooses—God will speak to you and prepare you for the things you will encounter. If you will linger with God, listening to Him in prayer and through the Word, you will hear all that you need to hear in order to live out your Christianity before a watching world. The key to hearing from the Lord is to come to Him with a heart that is seeking *His agenda* for your life and ministry.

Many times people approach God saying, "O God, please go with me this day and bless me!" God may say something like this to them: "You have it backwards! I have a will and a plan for what I want to do through your life today. I want *you* to go with *Me*; I want *you* to be a partner with *Me* today!"

During your quiet time, the Lord will bring to your heart His thoughts and plans. He will give you the full assurance that whatever

113

the Father has in mind, He will be present with you and in you to provide all the resources you need to see His will fulfilled through you. In addition, the Holy Spirit will be giving His assurance and will enable you to implement in your life this specific will of God. What an incredible privilege! What an awesome responsibility! What an accountability we have to love Him, believe Him, trust Him, and obey Him.

Let's look at an example of this truth: While you are reading the Bible, the Holy Spirit causes you to focus on Luke 12:12, "*For the Holy Spirit will teach you in that very hour what you ought to say.*" You meditate on this verse and, perhaps, write it down on a note card and put it in your pocket. As you go through the day, you meet a person who is visibly upset, and the Spirit reminds you of Luke 12:12. The Spirit has the opportunity to remind you of the verse because of your time spent with God that day. You silently pray for the Holy Spirit to teach you "*what you ought to say,*" and then He gives you the exact words this person needs to hear. You experience the wonderful presence and power of God working out His will in you and through you to help someone in need.

In moments like this, be sure to recognize that you are the instrument God chose to use to bring hope and encouragement to someone He deeply loves. Your life is a part of God's agenda! When you seek God and release your life to be available for His agenda, you can live expectantly, knowing that He will use your life to help others in need.

Lord, I want to know Your agenda for my life and be alert and ready to respond the moment You speak. Father, please show me Your plans and purposes for my life this week. In the name of Jesus, Amen.

DIGGING DEEPER
THROUGH THE WEEK

As you study the Bible and pray each day this week, ask God to give you His agenda. Pay careful attention to the verses He impresses on your heart as you study and pray. Write these verses down and meditate on them throughout the day.

At the end of your day, ask God to show you which situations He was working in and anticipate continuation of His work. Record the activity of God in your spiritual journal and review it often. Don't forget to thank God for using your life to accomplish His eternal purposes!

Experiencing Joy in the Call

*"Do not sorrow, for the joy of the LORD
is your strength."*

—Nehemiah 8:10

So often we look at the call of God on our lives and focus on the work ahead or the sacrifices involved. While much labor is involved and many sacrifices are made along the way, these things are as nothing when you look at the joy that comes from following the call of God. We experience the greatest joy when we know that we are exactly where God wants us to be—doing exactly what God wants us to do. When we hear His voice and see Him do things that can only be described as *God's activity*, our hearts are filled with unspeakable joy and peace. Watching His hand guide us each day brings excitement and a deep sense of purpose to our lives.

Jesus urged the disciples to remain or abide in His love by keeping His commandments (John 15:9–10; see also Week 2). As a result, they would remain in the love of the Father. He went on to say that the reason He was telling them to do this was so that His joy would remain in them and that their joy would be full. Jesus made it very clear how we can stay *full of joy*—through an abiding relationship of obedience and love with our heavenly Father:

"As the Father loved Me, I also have loved you; abide in My love. If you keep My commandments, you will abide in My love, just as I have kept My Father's commandments and abide in His love. These things I have spoken to you, that My joy may remain in you, and that your joy may be full."

—JOHN 15:9–11

When we follow God's directives in our lives and submit ourselves to His will, we experience the joy of Christ in abundance as a result.

Paul endured many hardships and difficulties in his ministry (2 Corinthians 11:22–33). However, when reading Paul's letters, we sense that, regardless of the pain and suffering he endured, he experienced great joy in his service to God (see Romans 15:13; 2 Corinthians 2:3; 2 Corinthians 7:4; 2 Corinthians 12:10; Philippians 1:4; Philemon 20). Resting in the joy of the Lord refreshes our hearts, motivates our lives, and changes our perspective on difficult circumstances. It changes our focus from our surroundings to our relationship with Christ and, in turn, renews our spirit.

In addition, great joy comes from living out the call in the midst of God's people. God has given us such a wonderful gift in the church! It is a place where believers gather to worship Him, to carry one another's burdens in prayer, and to proclaim and study the Word of God. When we think back over the times we have been overwhelmed with joy or excited because of something God had done, we remember that most often we could not wait to share the good news with our church family. An excitement is generated by serving God together as His called out people.

Great joy comes when we are on mission with God and with His people! And along with this joy comes a great fellowship and intimacy with God that serves to strengthen us to live out the call of God.

Heavenly Father, You are good; Your love and mercy bring such joy to my life. May I abide in Your love, and may I experience the fullness of Your joy today. Amen.

DIGGING DEEPER
THROUGH THE WEEK

In 1 Thessalonians 5:16–18, we are told, *"Rejoice always, pray without ceasing, in everything give thanks; for this is the will of God in Christ Jesus for you."* And in Nehemiah 8:10, we read that *"the joy of the LORD is your strength."* Oftentimes we face situations that are not joyful. The death of a loved one is a very painful experience. The loss of a job or a failure in life can cause great sorrow. In these verses, we are not told to rejoice *for* everything that happens to us. That is, we aren't expected to shout for joy when a death occurs or another type of devastating loss comes into our lives. However, we are told to *"rejoice always"* and to give thanks *in* everything. We don't thank God *for* the tragedy, but we do thank Him that *in the midst of tragedy,* He has given us the Holy Spirit, His Word, and the church to help us in our time of need.

Take time this week to rejoice in the Lord. Ask God to show you His perspective on your life and to help you remember all of the ways He has cared for you in the past. This will bring peace and joy to your life as you face circumstances that are difficult.

This week, ask God to grant you strength to live out your life with the joy!

Called to Understand

For we must all appear before the judgment seat of
Christ, that each one may receive the things done
in the body, according to what he has done,
whether good or bad.

—2 Corinthians 5:10

Have you been living your life with the understanding that one day, you will give an account for how you used your life, either in service to God or looking out for self? You see, you can't serve God and self at the same time. How has this understanding shaped the way you order your goals and priorities? The call of God is a call to an all-encompassing relationship with God. In this relationship, you must completely release your life to Him so He can accomplish His purposes through you.

God calls you by causing you to want to do His will; then He enables you to do it. He first calls you to be His child by faith in Jesus, His Son. A call to salvation is a call to be on mission with the Lord. At the moment of salvation, you enter into a relationship with Jesus in which He becomes your Lord and you become His servant. In that relationship, God provides all that is needed to live abundantly with Him. You will never have to look for a special or separate call of God to serve Him—the call is to obedience at the moment of salvation!

As a Christian, you are given one life to live. Have you released your life to God? Or are you holding back part of your life or resources? How tragic it would be to waste the opportunity to be a co-worker with Jesus Christ in your generation! As a Christian, answering the call of God brings joy and indescribable satisfaction to your heart. It also brings peace to your life and overcomes all your fears.

In what areas of your life have you seen God working this week? Has He invited you to join Him in His work? If not, you must take time to evaluate your relationship with Christ right now—don't wait another moment. If you are His child, He will invite you to work alongside Him in the world. If you have not heard from Him or paid attention to His activity around you, you are missing out!

You might say, "Well, my life is really busy right now, and I haven't had much time for Bible study or prayer." The busier you are, the more time you must spend with God in order to faithfully live out His call. Make adjustments in your life today so that you are spending an unhurried and uninterrupted time with the Lord each day. Ask Him to show you where He is working. Prepare your heart in advance to join Him in His work by answering, "Yes, Lord," to whatever assignment He gives.

Dear God, I want to live each moment on mission with You in this generation. I don't want to miss a single assignment or opportunity. Please open my understanding in a fresh way to where You are working around me and how I can join You today. In Jesus's name, Amen.

DIGGING DEEPER
THROUGH THE WEEK

This week, meditate on the following Scriptures in which Jesus describes His Father's work. Then apply each to your own life and relationship with God. Can you describe your relationship with God and your goals the same way Jesus does?

1. John 8:28–29, 38

2. John 4:34

3. John 14:10

THE CHARACTER OF THE CALLED: POOR IN SPIRIT

"Blessed are the poor in spirit, for theirs is the kingdom of heaven."

—MATTHEW 5:3

Persons who are *"poor in spirit"* recognize that they are completely and utterly "poor" in the realm of God. Understanding that spiritual needs cannot be filled apart from God, they are completely dependent on God to meet every need, want, and desire of their heart. These persons know that they have nothing to bring to God—except themselves.

In John 15:5, Jesus describes the believer's life as a branch attached to *Him*, the Vine, and then He makes this statement: *"Without Me you can do nothing."* The one who is really poor in spirit is the one who understands what Jesus meant by *"nothing."*

What does *nothing* mean to us? Does it mean that we can't do very much without Jesus? Or perhaps it means that we can do our jobs on our own, but not spiritual things? Maybe it could be said, "Without Jesus, we have a handicap or disability." A better understanding of the statement is this: "Without Jesus, we are hopelessly paralyzed." Without remaining *"in"* Him, we are hopelessly paralyzed and are of no use to God in the kingdom.

The ones who are poor in spirit are content to stay attached to the Vine, recognizing that all of their life decisions come through this relationship. They realize their absolute dependence on God and know that their only source of complete peace and rest is found in Him.

Isaiah 66:2 also gives a great picture of being poor in spirit: *"But to this one I will look, to him who is humble and contrite of spirit, and who trembles at My word"* (NASB).

Can you describe your character as *"humble and contrite"*? Would someone close to you describe you this way? To be humble, may we suggest, is to submit all of your opinions and all of your attitudes to God and, in turn, allow God's perspective to permeate your character.

What are you facing today? If you want to approach the situation with a poor-in-spirit attitude, then you must submit your will to God. Trust Him to do what He sees is best.

Finally, let's examine the result of being poor in spirit: The kingdom of heaven belongs to such persons. This is not a reward from God for having a character that is poor in spirit, but an automatic by-product of being poor in spirit. Those whose character is poor in spirit have the kingdom of heaven as their possession.

What does life look like for persons who possess the kingdom of heaven? Romans 14:17 states that their lives will be marked with *"righteousness and peace and joy in the Holy Spirit."*

Once we recognize that we have nothing to bring to God, and that without remaining in Him, we are hopelessly paralyzed, we will began to see our lives from God's perspective. This is the essence of being poor in spirit. When we see our lives from His viewpoint, submitting our wills to His, the entire kingdom of heaven is opened to us.

Heavenly Father, I lay all my opinions, beliefs, attitudes, and ideas about my life before You today. Please replace them with Your opinions, beliefs, attitudes, and ideas. In the name of Jesus, Amen.

DIGGING DEEPER
THROUGH THE WEEK

Take a few minutes this week to study Luke 5:1–11. As you read this account, consider the following questions:

1. How does Peter's response to Jesus show that he was poor in spirit?

2. When Peter responded with a heart that was poor in spirit, what did Jesus invite him to do?

Look back over the past month. How would you describe your dependence on God? How did your activities, decisions, plans, successes, and failures line up with Jesus' statement, *"Without Me you can do nothing"*?

The Character of the Called: Mournful

*"Blessed are those who mourn,
for they shall be comforted."*

—Matthew 5:4

The word *mourn* is not a pleasant word, but a sad word that describes a deep pain in the heart. When we hear it, the first thought is usually related to death. Yet we mourn for many reasons: death of a loved one, broken relationships, financial loss, tragedy in our world, and unsaved family or friends—and the list continues. When we reach the point of mourning over circumstances in our lives, we are usually in a very desperate place.

As we consider Jesus's words, we must ask for His perspective. We must ask the Holy Spirit to reveal what God-centered mourning looks like. Jesus had just stated, as recorded in the previous verse, that persons who are *"poor in spirit"* hold the keys to the kingdom of heaven in their hands. Then His next words discussed mourning. *So what is God-centered mourning?*

God-centered mourning is a deep grief over sin in our lives or in the lives of those around us. While it is true that God comforts those who mourn over the death of a loved one, Jesus was not discussing that issue here. Rather, He was saying, "Blessed are those who are poor in spirit, who recognize their helpless state and who grieve or mourn over their sin." Paul says it like this in Romans 7:

> *For I know that in me (that is, in my flesh) nothing good dwells; for to will is present with me, but how to perform what is good I do not find. For the good that I will to do, I do not do; but the evil I will not to do, that I practice. Now if I do what I will not to do, it is no longer I who do it, but sin that dwells in me. I find then a law, that evil is present with me, the one who wills to do good. For I delight in the law of God according to the inward man. But I see another law in my members, warring against the law of my mind, and bringing me into captivity to the law of sin which is in my members. O wretched man that I am! Who will deliver me from this body of death? I thank God—through Jesus Christ our Lord!*
>
> —ROMANS 7:18–25

When we see our sin from God's perspective, we are deeply grieved. Often, we might feel like Paul, in that a battle is raging within us. Although we will to do good, we sometimes fail. As we recognize this, a deep sense of grief over our sin comes upon us. However, we can *"thank God—through Jesus Christ our Lord,"* who will forgive us, thus bringing the comfort Jesus promised to those who mourn. We will see ourselves as the prophet Isaiah saw himself and said, *"Woe is me, for I am undone! Because I am a man of unclean lips, and I dwell in the midst of a people of unclean lips; for my eyes have seen the King, the LORD of hosts"* (Isaiah 6:5).

Why do you think Jesus said that *"those who mourn"* are *"blessed"*? They are blessed because they will *"be comforted"*—they will have immediate and unlimited access to the Holy Spirit, our Comforter!

Mourning over our sin creates a dependence on God. This dependence on God keeps our hearts sensitive to Him and allows us to live out the call of God.

Lord, I thank You for providing the Comforter to me.
As I reflect on my life and the many times I have sinned
this week, I pray that You forgive me and fill me with
Your presence. May my fellowship with You grow more
intimate each day. Through this relationship, keep me
from sin and continuously draw me closer to You.
Lord, help me remain dependent upon You, so
I will honor You in my daily walk. Amen.

 ## DIGGING DEEPER
THROUGH THE WEEK

Many times when we experience deep loss or seasons of grief, we turn to the Psalms for comfort and help. Psalm 51 is David's prayer of repentance after his sin with Bathsheba. Take time this week to read this psalm several times and reflect on the following questions:

1. What was David's first request (v. 1)?

2. How did he describe his sin in his prayer to God (vv. 3–4)?

3. What requests did David make as he continued his prayer of repentance (vv. 2, 7–12, 14)?

4. As king, David could have prepared an extravagant burnt offering or sacrifice. However, what did David describe in this prayer as preferred or acceptable offerings to God (vv. 16–17)?

THE CHARACTER OF THE CALLED: MEEK

"Blessed are the meek, for they shall inherit the earth."

—MATTHEW 5:5

The word *meekness* is often confused with the word *weakness*. The illustration of a well-trained horse will help describe the characteristics of meek persons. The horse is a large, powerful animal. It has ability to overpower many creatures, including human beings, with ease. It can use its strength any way it chooses—when it is unbridled. However, when a trained rider saddles and bridles a horse, the strength of the horse is transferred into the hands of its rider. The horse is still powerful, but its strength is under the control of its master—and that is when the horse is useful. Meekness is the same; it is power under control. In the same way, individuals are useful to God when their lives are fully controlled by Him.

Regardless of whether individuals are weak or strong, they must still submit to and depend on God. Meekness *can* be a characteristic of persons with very strong personalities—if they choose not to assert themselves, but, rather, submit their wills to God.

Meekness and humility are similar. Having a humble spirit is when every response of the heart is directed to the Lord, and the

Holy Spirit is allowed to respond for an individual. Humility is not controlled by circumstances; rather humility controls a person's response to the circumstances—it's how the person responds in his or her heart to the situation.

Jesus said over and over again that He spoke and acted only according to what His Father told Him to say or do. Notice that in John 8:38, He said something like this: "I'm revealing in words what I saw while spending time in My Father's presence" (paraphrased). And in John 14:24, He states, *"The word which you hear is not Mine but the Father's who sent Me."*

David had an understanding of this secret and, in Psalm 19:14, he prayed, *"Let the words of my mouth and the meditation of my heart be acceptable in Your sight, O LORD, my strength and my Redeemer."* Again, in Psalm 37:11, he said, *"But the meek shall inherit the earth and shall delight themselves in the abundance of peace."*

Those who are meek have learned to submit their thoughts, plans, opinions, and wills to the Father's. They have no opinion on the outcome of their lives because they have put their lives into His hands and released their wills to Him.

This teaching is radically different from what the world teaches. The world will tell us to be self-assertive, but in the end, it is the meek, not the self-assertive, who will inherit the earth.

Dear Lord, I give my life to You today—releasing my will to Yours, trusting You to do what You see is best in Your kingdom and in this earth. In Jesus's name, Amen.

DIGGING DEEPER
THROUGH THE WEEK

Prayerfully think about this past week, and reflect upon activities in which you participated. Try to remember the people you encountered and the conversations you shared together. How many times did you find yourself in a situation in which your response was characterized as meek?

As you responded to people or circumstances, did you find your life to be controlled by the hand of God, or were your activities and words the result of your own opinion and desires?

THE CHARACTER OF THE CALLED: HUNGRY AND THIRSTY FOR RIGHTEOUSNESS

"Blessed are those who hunger and thirst for righteousness, for they shall be filled."

—MATTHEW 5:6

When we are hungry or thirsty during the day, we usually stop and get something to eat or drink. Our need is satisfied quickly, and we continue about our day. But can you remember a time when you were really hungry but couldn't eat or thirsty and didn't have a drink? Maybe after working outside or after a long jog, you have been desperate for a refreshing drink. The feeling is intense, isn't it?

We can't live very long without food or drink. Going without basic nourishment for long periods makes us weak and unable to function at full capacity. After a while, our thoughts turn toward eating and drinking. We are consumed with one intent: satisfying our craving.

When we *"hunger and thirst for righteousness,"* we long intensely after righteousness. The only thing that will satisfy us is being in right standing with God. It is not simply *doing* what is right; it is a passionate concern for *being* right—inside and out.

131

What is righteousness? Is it feeling good about ourselves or having our friends, family, and co-workers think we are good persons? Those are good things, but they are not righteousness. Righteousness is being in right standing with God. This righteousness is not something that we will one day achieve—it is given to us by the Father through Jesus's death and resurrection. We are not *"blessed"* by our *achievement of righteousness,* because righteousness is not something that is accomplished in our own strength. But we are blessed because we want nothing more than to be right with God. This is an intense focus on hungering and thirsting to be in right standing with God. It brings satisfaction and contentment to our whole being. Our part is to hunger and thirst for it, to keep it as our most intense craving; then God will fill us.

Jesus summed it up in Matthew 6:33: *"But seek first the kingdom of God and **His righteousness,** and all these things shall be added to you"* (boldface added for emphasis). Notice the word *added.* This word indicates God will add to what He has already given you. It gives us the picture of an ongoing process of adding or filling, which results in continually having enough or being satisfied. Being satisfied is the most wonderful place we can be as Christians. As we seek—search or long intensely for—God's kingdom and His righteousness, God will continually fill our lives, meeting every need.

This hunger for being right with God and His continual filling of our lives will keep us on track in living out the call of God.

*Heavenly Father, I desire many things, but only one
thing do I really need: to seek first Your kingdom and
Your righteousness. Father, may my focus in life
be continually set on being right with You.
In Jesus's name, Amen.*

DIGGING DEEPER
THROUGH THE WEEK

Are you hungry? Is something missing from your life? Are you dissatisfied or weak in your relationship with Christ? Ask yourself this question: "What am I longing for?" If your answer is not, "Righteousness," then refocus your life on the Lord and make your aim to be right with Him. He, in turn, will satisfy and fill your deepest needs.

The Character of the Called: Merciful

"Blessed are the merciful, for they shall obtain mercy."

—Matthew 5:7

Mercy is used many times in the Old Testament to describe God. In fact, God describes Himself as merciful in Exodus 34:6–7: *"And the LORD passed before him and proclaimed, 'The LORD, the LORD God, merciful and gracious, longsuffering, and abounding in goodness and truth, keeping mercy for thousands, forgiving iniquity and transgression and sin.'"*

The mercy and grace of God are often used in conjunction with each other; however, they have very different meanings. *Grace* is God giving us what we don't deserve; *mercy* is God withholding what we do deserve.

Jesus says those who are merciful will receive or be shown mercy. Turning that thought around suggests this: Those who do not show mercy will not be shown mercy. It is very important to ask God to show us if we are known by Him to be merciful.

How would you know if you are characterized by God as a person who is merciful? In Luke 6:45, Jesus says, *"A good man out of the good treasure of his heart brings forth good; and an evil man out of*

*the evil treasure of his heart brings forth evil. For out of the abundance of
the heart his mouth speaks."*

Now rephrase this verse using the words *merciful* or *mercy* for
good, and *unmerciful* or *no mercy* for *evil:*

> A *merciful* man out of the *merciful* treasure of his heart
> brings forth *mercy*; and an *unmerciful* man out of the
> *unmerciful* treasure of his heart brings forth *no mercy*. For
> out of the abundance of the heart his mouth speaks.

Now ask yourself what your tendency or bent is as you relate to
other people. Is it to show mercy to your spouse, your children, your
co-workers, and your mother-in-law? Or is the evidence of *mercy* in
your life sporadic or an occasional impulse when you are in a good
mood? Ask yourself this question: "What is my first thought when
someone is unkind to me?" Is your heart filled with mercy? If so,
then out of the abundance of your heart, your mouth will speak.
Notice that Jesus doesn't say that your mouth *might* speak, but that
your mouth *speaks* exactly what is in your heart.

If God is revealing to you that your heart is not filled with
mercy, what should you do? Ask Him to show you the reason.

If you are merciful, you will be shown or will receive mercy.
If mercy flows from your life to those around you, the channel for
you to receive mercy will be open and flowing. However, if the
flow of mercy from you is closed or blocked with unforgiveness,
the channel for you to receive mercy will be closed.

In living out God's call, you will walk alongside other people,
some of whom will be an encouragement to you, while some will
push you to "go deeper" with God. But walking alongside others
always brings challenges. We all have room to grow and, thus, *need*
mercy; so we need to be prepared to *show* mercy to others.

*Merciful Lord, You have shown me mercy and
poured out Your grace over my life more times than
I can possibly comprehend. Thank You for Your mercy.
Father, make me a merciful person. Help my heart
to be filled with kindness and love for those You
have placed around me and for those You bring into
my life today. In Jesus's name, Amen.*

DIGGING DEEPER
THROUGH THE WEEK

Take time to prayerfully reflect on the past few days. Ask the Lord
to show you if you have been merciful to these persons in your life:

- Parents

- Spouse

- Children

- Co-workers

- Neighbors

- Church family

- Enemies

The Character of the Called: Pure in Heart

"Blessed are the pure in heart, for they shall see God."
—Matthew 5:8

Oh, to have clean hands and a pure heart! Our lives would have unhindered access to God; we would see God in every circumstance and everywhere we turn.

What does Jesus mean by *"pure in heart"*? It means having pure thoughts, pure motives, a pure will, and pure emotions. God requires purity at the very center of our being, in our heart. David said it this way in Psalm 24:

> *Who may ascend into the hill of the LORD? Or who may stand in His holy place? He who has clean hands and a pure heart, who has not lifted up his soul to an idol, nor sworn deceitfully. He shall receive blessing from the LORD, and righteousness from the God of his salvation.*

—Psalm 24:3–6

Several years ago, we had a family reunion in England. It was a wonderful time that provided incredible memories. While in London, we had the opportunity to tour Buckingham Palace. We saw the London Guard, beautiful tapestries, and other artwork and paintings from world-renowned artists. We walked in the hallways and stood in the rooms where history had been made. We were fascinated by the London Guard. Our tour guide told us that the highest military honor is to be assigned to guard Queen Elizabeth and Buckingham Palace. As we watched the changing of the Guard, we noticed that the guards marched, stood, and were dressed perfectly. The Queen has only the best of the best serving at her palace.

What king or queen would have someone with filthy hands serving at his or her table? In our wildest imagination, we can't picture a queen having someone dirty to serve her. It would be unacceptable. If a servant came to work unclean, he or she would be ineligible to attend to the queen's personal needs. In the same way, Jesus—the King of kings—requires that those who serve Him have clean hands and pure hearts.

Jesus said those who have pure hearts will see God; they will sit around His table and serve Him. They will hear what He says, know what is on His heart for the day, and see where He is working.

Many times we want to see God's activity and to be a part of His work in our world, but we don't seem to see Him do much through our lives. We wonder where He is and why He hasn't spoken to us or shown us His plans. If you have wondered the same thing, take a moment to consider your life. Are you ready for service? Are your hands clean from any stain of sin, and are the motives of your heart pure? Perhaps you need to pray as David did in Psalm 51:

> *Create in me a clean heart, O God, and renew a steadfast spirit within me. Do not cast me away from Your presence, and do not take Your Holy Spirit from me. Restore to me the joy of Your salvation, and uphold me by Your generous Spirit.*
>
> —PSALM 51:10–12

Father, I join David in praying: "How can I know all the sins lurking in my heart? Cleanse me from these hidden faults. Keep your servant from deliberate sins! Don't let them control me.... May the words of my mouth and the meditation of my heart be pleasing to you, O LORD, my rock and my redeemer" (Psalm 19:12–14 NLT). In the name of Jesus, Amen.

DIGGING DEEPER
THROUGH THE WEEK

As you strive to attain or maintain a pure heart, consider the following questions:

1. How well have you guarded your heart?

2. What are you allowing your eyes to see and your ears to hear?

3. Do you have a clean life?

4. What protective means have you put in place in your life to ensure that your heart and hands stay clean so that your service to the Lord is unhindered?

5. Those who have clean hands and pure hearts *will* see God. Are you seeing and experiencing God working in and through your life?

6. Are you sitting before the Lord, watching and listening carefully for your assignments each day?

7. What assignments has God given you this week?

WEEK 44

THE CHARACTER OF THE CALLED: PEACEMAKER

"Blessed are the peacemakers, for they shall be called sons of God."

—MATTHEW 5:9

If you take time to read Matthew 5:1–12, you will notice that all of the Beatitudes build on each other. This one is no different. To be a peacemaker, we must have a heart that is poor in spirit and one that mourns over sin. We must be people who are meek, hungering for God's wisdom and righteousness. We must be merciful and have clean hands and a pure heart if we really want to be a peacemaker.

In our day, we see many people who are trying to "keep the peace." However, there is a vast difference between a *peacekeeper* and a *peacemaker*.

A peacekeeper is one who strives to keep the peace so that everything is balanced and smooth. This person will say, "Peace, peace," when there is no peace. But this offers no resolution—just quietness for the moment.

A peacemaker is very different. This person desires to bring an end to the difficulty or conflict by bringing those in conflict to reconciliation with God and each other. A peacemaker overcomes evil with good (Romans 12:21) and promotes peace. A peacemaker

140

is one who is in tune with God and one whom God can use as an instrument of reconciliation. Jesus is the ultimate example of this truth. His life clearly displayed all of the Beatitudes, and He was the instrument God used to bring reconciliation to the world.

Peacemakers don't simply "put out fires" just to keep the peace; they speak the truth in love (Ephesians 4:15), which brings life and peace to God's people. In the middle of a conflict or disagreement, sin is present in both parties. Peacemakers help people see their sin—sin against God and other persons. Peacemakers bring life and hope to difficult situations, quite like Jesus's obedience brought eternal life to us.

The result of being a peacemaker is very special: *"they shall be called sons of God."* Wow! Persons whose lives are marked as *peacemakers* or *reconcilers* have a very special place in God's family. They have entered into a special relationship with God in which He calls them His own child!

We strive to teach our children to hear and follow God. When a child "acts" the right way and makes choices that are in harmony with his or her parents' beliefs, the parents are usually very proud and not ashamed to say, "This is my child." They want everyone to know that their child made the right choice and honored the parents. In the same way, Jesus says, "Those who are peacemakers will be called sons of God." That is, God is pleased, not ashamed, to call the peacemaker His child.

What are you facing right now? Are you experiencing difficulties in your family or within your church? If conflict is surrounding you, God is looking to use one of His children to bring an end to the conflict. Could He be giving you this special assignment?

Heavenly Father, I confess that sometimes I would rather look away from conflict than get involved. If You are calling me to be a peacemaker in any area, please show me, and I will be faithful to obey. Amen.

DIGGING DEEPER
THROUGH THE WEEK

James 3 gives us instructions on getting along with others. In the *Amplified Bible,* James describes the wisdom from above as being *"peace-loving."* Further, he gives us an illustration of a *"harvest of righteousness"* that comes by sowing peace in ourselves and in others:

> But the wisdom from above is first of all pure (undefiled); then it is peace-loving, courteous (considerate, gentle). [It is willing to] yield to reason, full of compassion and good fruits; it is wholehearted and straightforward, impartial and unfeigned (free from doubts, wavering, and insincerity). And the harvest of righteousness (of conformity to God's will in thought and deed) is [the fruit of the seed] sown in peace by those who work for and make peace [in themselves and in others, that peace which means concord, agreement, and harmony between individuals, with undisturbedness, in a peaceful mind free from fears and agitating passions and moral conflicts].
>
> —JAMES 3:17–18 (AMP)

Take time this week to read chapters 3 and 4 of the Book of James. Meditate on the instructions he gives regarding sowing peace and being a person who loves peace. Ask God to show you if you are walking in the wisdom from above.

The Character of the Called: Enduring Persecution

"Blessed are those who are persecuted for righteousness' sake, for theirs is the kingdom of heaven. Blessed are you when they revile and persecute you, and say all kinds of evil against you falsely for My sake. Rejoice and be exceedingly glad, for great is your reward in heaven, for so they persecuted the prophets who were before you."

—Matthew 5:10–12

At the end of the Beatitudes, Jesus explains that we are blessed through persecution. He says we are blessed when people insult us and persecute us and falsely accuse us. He goes on to say that we should rejoice and be glad about it. He gives us two ideas about this blessing: One is that we are blessed in the here and now; and the other is that we are blessed (or rewarded) in heaven, or in the future.

Notice that we are blessed when persecuted *"for righteousness' sake."* What does Jesus mean by the phrase *for righteousness' sake*? He is very specific when He discusses being blessed through persecution. We are not blessed when we are persecuted for just any reason, but we are blessed when we because of our right standing with God and our diligence in obeying Him are persecuted. Just as those who are poor in spirit will possess *"the kingdom of heaven,"* those who are *"persecuted for righteousness' sake"* will have as their possession *"the kingdom of heaven."*

In 2 Timothy 3, Paul explained that difficult times will come for the righteous—for those who are in right standing with God:

> *But you have carefully followed my doctrine, manner of life, purpose, faith, longsuffering, love, perseverance, persecutions, afflictions, which happened to me at Antioch, at Iconium, at Lystra—what persecutions I endured. And out of them all the Lord delivered me. Yes, and all who desire to live godly in Christ Jesus will suffer persecution. But evil men and impostors will grow worse and worse, deceiving and being deceived. But you must continue in the things which you have learned and been assured of, knowing from whom you have learned them, and that from childhood you have known the Holy Scriptures, which are able to make you wise for salvation through faith which is in Christ Jesus.*
>
> —2 Timothy 3:10–15

A key to being blessed in the midst of persecution is to bear in mind all the things God has done for you in the past. *Remember* how He has cared for you, provided for you, blessed you, and encouraged you. *Remember* that He promises never to leave you or forsake you. *Remember* what He has done in history through other believers, and especially *remember* what He has done and revealed through His Word.

Hebrews 12:1–11 is always a helpful passage to read in the middle of persecutions or difficult situations. In particular, note verse 11: *"Now no chastening seems to be joyful for the present but painful;*

nevertheless, afterward it yields the peaceable fruit of righteousness to those who have been trained by it" (Hebrews 12:11).

Persecution is painful, but we can be blessed in the middle of it because we have access to the One and Only who can comfort us, give perfect wisdom, fight for us, and defend us.

Heavenly Father, as I face many difficulties in my life, please give me the courage to walk through them in a way that brings honor to Your name. Bring to my remembrance all of the ways You have guided and protected me in the past so that I won't stumble in this present situation. I love You, Lord. Amen.

DIGGING DEEPER
THROUGH THE WEEK

When we forget the wonderful things God has shown us and done for us, we are in danger. Take time right now to *remember* the many blessings God has given you. Think back over the last year, and ask the Holy Spirit to bring to your remembrance the wonderful ways God has blessed you and your family. Then spend some time thinking about your life and how God has kept His hand on you and cared for you. Write down the things or circumstances the Holy Spirit brings to mind. Spend time thanking God for His goodness.

Take time to meditate on Hebrews 12:1–11 this week, and memorize verses 3 through 6.

Accountable to Forgive

Then Peter came to Him and said, "Lord, how often shall my brother sin against me, and I forgive him? Up to seven times?" Jesus said to him, "I do not say to you, up to seven times, but up to seventy times seven."

—Matthew 18:21–22

Following the call of God means that there will be times in our lives when we encounter enemies. Most of us have had the opportunity to turn the other cheek or to extend forgiveness to someone who wronged us. We need to receive forgiveness each day; and most days, we experience situations in which we need to extend forgiveness to others. We might not have what we would call "major" things happen in our lives each day that require us to forgive, but often just "little" things occur.

For example, if you live with someone, that person has probably, at times, left dirty dishes around the house. Or if you are married, your spouse may have said something that hurt you, or maybe he or she didn't do something important that you asked. Maybe your children "forgot" to complete a chore, which, in turn, caused you to be late for work. On the other hand, maybe something major has happened to you. Has your best friend walked away from you, and you don't understand why? Perhaps one of your grown children won't communicate with you or return your phone calls. Has anyone ever told a lie about you, borrowed money from you without paying it back, or stolen material goods from you? All of these things require you to forgive.

Jesus makes it clear to us that we must forgive others because our forgiveness of others is associated with God's forgiveness of us. We need to forgive others the same way we want Him to forgive us (Matthew 6:12, 14–15). In Matthew 5:38–48, Jesus says that He not only wants us to forgive those who wrong us, but He wants us to love them and to be kind to them so they will have the chance to know someone like Himself, to know a child of God (v. 45). Jesus says that we are acting just like the world (the darkness—those who don't know Him) if we love only those who love us. He sets a high standard for His followers, challenging them to *be right* in their hearts rather than simply *acting right* by obeying the Law, for example, the Ten Commandments.

So if we are not to defend ourselves, who will defend us? In Romans 12:19, Paul wrote, *"leave the way open for [God's] wrath"* (AMP). Leaving our enemies in God's hands changes everything. If we defend ourselves, we receive the best defense *we* can give. However, if we let God defend us, we get *God's* best defense.

Settle in your heart ahead of time to forgive, because extending forgiveness is inevitable as you live out the call of God on your life.

*Heavenly Father, I want to deal with my enemies
according to Your Word and through the power of
Your Holy Spirit. Give me wisdom daily to turn
the other cheek and to love all those whom
You have placed in my path. Amen.*

DIGGING DEEPER
THROUGH THE WEEK

Read John 12:1–8, and answer the following questions:

1. How did Mary respond to Judas's criticism?

2. Who defended Mary?

Jesus defended Mary, and He did it in such a way that Mary didn't have to say a word. She continued serving the Lord and wasn't distracted by her enemy.

We see Mary responded the same way in Luke 10:38–42. In this passage, Martha was angry with Mary for not helping her serve Jesus and the disciples. In this situation also, Jesus defended Mary. And once again, Mary kept her mouth shut and her heart set on obedience. Oh, what a lesson for us to learn!

CALLED TO BE SALT

"You are the salt of the earth."
—MATTHEW 5:13

Salt is used for a variety of purposes every day. When used in food as a flavoring or preservative, salt isn't seen; but we know it's there, because we experience its flavor. In this case, salt does its work subtly. However, when salt is used as an antiseptic, it is not subtle but painfully noticeable.

In Jesus's day, salt was a necessity. It had many uses: It served as a catalyst to get an oven started. It was used as a fertilizer to improve the quality of the soil. On the other hand, in large amounts, salt poured on weeds served as a weed killer. It was also used as a preservative to keep food from decay, since no refrigeration system was available during that time.

What did Jesus have in mind when He made the statement, *"You are the salt of the earth"*? He might have wanted the disciples to be catalysts for starting and spreading the fire of the gospel. He could have been thinking about how His disciples could be used to improve the quality of the lives of those with whom they came into contact and, thus, produce more and better fruit. Perhaps He wanted His disciples to be used as agents for fighting off spiritual decay and the infection of sin. He may have also wanted them to add zest to the lives they touched. Consuming salty foods creates thirst; Jesus wanted His disciples' character and conduct to make people thirsty for Him and the salvation that He alone could give them. These are many different ideas on what Jesus may have meant when He said, "*You are the salt of the earth.*" Most of these examples can be easily applied to our lives.

We must remember one thing in particular: Salt is valuable only when it comes in contact with something and, in turn, gives of itself. Salt is no good if it stays in its container; it must come in direct contact with something else for it to be valuable.

Notice what Jesus said, "*You **are** the salt of the earth.*" He didn't say that we should be the salt or that it would be nice if we acted like salt once in a while. He didn't make a suggestion; He stated a fact. He stated that we—everyday people—are the salt. We are in the world; we can't make a choice to move out of the world. So while we are on earth as Christians, we are to be salt. And we must keep ourselves in a right relationship with God so He can sprinkle us on or around any person or situation He chooses.

We are salt. We need to spend time meditating on this truth until we begin to anticipate opportunities and recognize how God is using us to be salt in our world each day.

Jesus challenges His followers to live out their lives in front of a watching world so the world will see what a relationship with God is like. When lost persons encounter Christians who are allowing Christ to use them as salt, the lost will see God and desire a relationship with Him. Are you allowing Christ to sprinkle your life on persons around you, particularly those who He knows are hurting?

 Heavenly Father, use me today to be salt in this world. Help me to be prepared and ready to be of maximum use to You. In the name of Jesus, Amen.

DIGGING DEEPER
THROUGH THE WEEK

As you consider the numerous uses for salt, prayerfully ask God to show you at least three times in the past month He used your life as salt.

When you were in the middle of these situations, did you realize that God was using your life as salt to bring healing or to preserve a life or maybe even to be a catalyst to start a fire?

CALLED TO BE LIGHT

*"You are the light of the world. A city that
is set on a hill cannot be hidden. Nor do they
light a lamp and put it under a basket, but on
a lampstand, and it gives light to all who are in
the house. Let your light so shine before men,
that they may see your good works and
glorify your Father in heaven."*

—MATTHEW 5:14–16

Children love to play with flashlights. Do you remember how much fun it was as a child to go into a dark room and turn on the flashlight? It could be pointed in any direction and on any thing and immediately illuminate that area. Flashlights are not only fun but also useful. We keep one in our car for emergencies; we keep one in the kitchen in case the electricity goes out; and we always take one on camping trips. While flashlights are used in a variety of places, they are always used for one purpose: to bring light to a dark place.

Have you ever tried to turn on a flashlight, only to find out the batteries were dead? Is a flashlight useful to you without batteries? No, it's not.

In John 8:12, Jesus says, *"I am the light of the world. He who follows Me shall not walk in darkness, but have the light of life."* As we consider Jesus's words, we are reminded that Jesus is the Light and that He, through the Holy Spirit, dwells within those of us who are Christians. He is the Light within us, and He wants to use our lives to bring light into the darkness around us.

Imagine yourself as a flashlight and your relationship with Jesus as the batteries. Your fellowship with Jesus is the source and sustainer of your light. Jesus holds you, the flashlight, in His hands so that He can direct and shine His light through you onto any person or situation He chooses. He can use you as a light in your neighborhood, your workplace, or your family. As long as the batteries are good, the flashlight is useful. However, if the batteries are corroded or dead, the flashlight is of no use.

In the same way, if we are out of fellowship with God, our lives (flashlights) are of no use in the kingdom of God. If corrosion is a problem, our batteries must be cleaned; if low on charge, they need to be recharged or replaced. In other words, in order to be the light of the world, we must be in a healthy, right relationship with Jesus so He can use us to shine His light into the darkness of this world.

As Jesus tells His disciples that they are the light of the world, He paints a wonderful word picture of a city sitting on a hill. When we are driving at night, the sight of a city on a hill is beautiful. The lights bring color and beauty to the night sky. As we approach the city, our eyes are drawn to the city lights; the lights become our focus because they dispel the darkness. The light of the city set on a hill will draw people to the city. Jesus tells His disciples that they are just like that city and that He will use them to draw the watching world to Himself. They will shine like lights in darkness for the purpose of drawing all people to God.

Lord, please give me the courage to let You
place me in the middle of the darkness to shine as
a light. May I not fear a dark place, but trust You
to illuminate my world by shining Your perfect
light through me today. Amen.

DIGGING DEEPER
THROUGH THE WEEK

Has God used your life to dispel darkness? Have you noticed God placing you in situations where there is no light of Christ?

Set aside some time this week to pray, asking God to show you how and where He wants to use your life to bring light in your home, your workplace, and your neighborhood. Once He reveals His plans to you, set aside 15 minutes each day to pray for these individuals and situations. Ask Him to fill, equip, and use your life as light.

Called to Ask, Seek, and Knock

*"Ask, and it will be given to you; seek,
and you will find; knock, and it will be opened
to you. For everyone who asks receives,
and he who seeks finds, and to him
who knocks it will be opened."*

—Matthew 7:7–8

Jesus does not give us specific instructions on how to ask. He just tells us that we must ask. He promises that when we do, our prayer will be effective: "*It will be given*" to them who ask.

Jesus does not tell us how to seek, but tells us that we should seek. Seeking is an intense asking. It isn't the idea that we do not know where to find what we are looking for. If that were the case, we wouldn't be praying. It is the idea of continually making God aware of our needs. When we do, we *"will find"* the answer. For a second time, we notice that answer to prayer is certain.

Knocking gives us the picture of someone standing in front of a closed door that cannot be opened. This person does not know how to open the door. It seems impossible. It is a picture of passionate seeking and a continual asking. Jesus says, "Knock, and the door will be opened." Again we see a greater level of intensity in prayer and a promise that it will be answered. We see this verse clearly explained in Jeremiah 29:13: *"You will seek Me and find Me, when you search for Me with all your heart."*

Why do you think Jesus uses these repetitions? He is encouraging a confident expectation of answered prayer in His disciples' lives. He is saying, "Don't give up!" In addition, He is emphasizing God's willingness to answer their prayers.

How do you pray? Have you been praying for a merciful heart? Jesus says, "Don't give up if you have an unmerciful thought or action." Keep on asking, seeking, and knocking. God will certainly answer this prayer.

Have you been praying for a loving attitude? Don't give up on letting God shape you into a loving person. Keep on asking, seeking, and knocking. God will, without fail, answer this prayer.

Have you been praying that you would be more patient with your family? Don't give up if you sin by being impatient with your children. Keep on asking, seeking, and knocking. God is more than willing to answer this prayer!

Has a little child ever asked you for something while you were shopping, and you simply said, "No, not today"? If a child accepts that type of answer and a simple no pacifies him or her, what conclusion do you draw? You think the child doesn't really want the requested item or maybe it really isn't very important to the child.

What if that same little child makes a request but doesn't want to take no for an answer and respectfully implores again for the item? You can tell by the look on the child's face that the desire for the item is intense. What conclusion do you draw? You might conclude that the child is determined and the item is important to that child. As a loving parent you will either grant the request or help the child understand that the item is not in his or her best interest at this time.

As we consider Jesus's teaching on asking, seeking, and knocking, we can apply it in many ways to our lives. We see that Jesus wants us to keep asking, keep seeking, and keep knocking with our requests. Whether we are asking to be *"poor in spirit"* or asking for the healing of a loved one, the message here is that we should continue asking, seeking, and knocking until God answers by granting our requests or showing us another way to pray.

 Heavenly Father, help me to be steadfast in my prayers to You. Lord, teach me to pray! In Jesus's name, Amen.

Digging Deeper
THROUGH THE WEEK

When studying a passage like Matthew 7:7–8, seeing an example of someone living out the truths described can sometimes be helpful. Let's look at a biblical example of this passage being "lived out" through the life of a very desperate mother. Read Matthew 15:21–28, and then answer the following questions:

1. How does the woman address Jesus (v. 22)?

2. What is she *asking* Jesus to do (v. 22)?

3. How does Jesus respond to her asking (v. 23)?

4. How do the disciples respond to her asking (v. 23)?

5. Next we see her request become more intense as her *seeking* is described in verse 25. What does she seek from Jesus (v. 25)?

6. How does Jesus respond to her seeking (v. 26; see also Mark 7:27)?

7. She continues her pleading in verse 27. Notice her understanding of Jesus's words and her humility in her *"knocking,"* so to speak (v. 27). How does Jesus respond to her knocking (v. 28)?

Here are some characteristics demonstrated in this woman's prayer:

- Her determination

- Her love for her daughter

- Her humility in approaching Jesus (She requested, "Have mercy on me.")

- Her willingness to take a risk by approaching Jesus both as a *woman* and as a *Syrophoenician* (Mark 7:26)

- Her pure heart (Even when Jesus *"answered her not a word,"* her automatic response was to worship Him.)

What characteristics does Jesus see in your life as you pray?

Accountable for Readiness

Again, the next day, John stood with two of his disciples. And looking at Jesus as He walked, he said, "Behold the Lamb of God!" The two disciples heard him speak, and they followed Jesus.

—John 1:35–37

John the Baptist is known as the forerunner to Christ. In that role, he prepared the way for Christ by pointing everyone he encountered to Jesus. John's message was, more or less, this: Get ready because the promised Messiah is coming!

In John 1:35–51, we see a wonderful picture of Jesus calling His first disciples. At the first of this passage, we see John the Baptist with two of his disciples. John made a statement—*"Behold the Lamb of God!"*—and his disciples dropped everything, left John, and followed after Christ. These men had heard about Christ but had never met Him. Yet we are told, *"They followed Jesus."* The word *followed* holds a deep meaning. It gives the picture of a once-and-for-all action or decision or the idea of casting their lot with Jesus. These men were looking for the Messiah, and as soon as they saw Him, they dropped everything and followed Him. How much convincing do you need to follow after Christ—to forsake all and follow Him?

It is worth noting that these men had already committed themselves to Christ before Jesus spoke to them. When Jesus turned to them and asked them a simple question, *"What do you seek?"* the text indicates that they didn't really know. The disciples replied, *"Where are You staying?"* indicating that they wanted to be with Him. Have you ever been there with the Lord? Maybe you have prayed, "Lord, I'm not sure what I need to ask or say, but I want to spend time with You." Or perhaps you may be facing a difficult circumstance and you need understanding; you know that if you could just spend enough time before the Lord, you would find the answers.

Jesus gave a wonderful response to the disciples' *"Where are You staying?"* question: *"Come and see."* He was saying to them, "Join Me; come and visit with Me; let's sit down and talk." We don't know what they talked about, but we see the response of Andrew after their visit. He immediately brought his brother Peter to Jesus. This is the natural response of a disciple of Christ—to bring others to Him. He didn't do it out of a sense of obligation, but because he did not want his brother to miss out on meeting the Christ.

This story is a wonderful picture of a relationship with Jesus. It is provided not simply for information, but for us to recognize that this same thing can happen in our lives if we follow the example of these disciples. Remember, they were looking for Christ before He even came by. When they recognized Him, they did not hesitate, but immediately committed their lives to follow Him. Further, they did not put conditions on the relationship, but asked only, *"Where are You staying?"* If we follow their example, we will hear the Lord say to us, *"Come and see"*!

Dear Lord, as I read this story of the early disciples,
I want to have the same fellowship with You.
Wherever You are staying is where I want to be.
Help me to recognize You immediately and
have everything in my life "ready"
for following You. Amen.

DIGGING DEEPER
THROUGH THE WEEK

Read John 1:35–51, and answer the following questions:

1. What was John the Baptist's response to Jesus, the Christ?

2. How did John's disciples respond to Christ?

3. What commitment did the disciples make?

4. How did Jesus respond to the disciples?

5. In light of this passage, what promise would you say Jesus makes to those who become His disciples?

CALLED BY THE COMPELLING LOVE OF CHRIST

For the love of Christ compels us, because we judge thus: that if One died for all, then all died; and He died for all, that those who live should live no longer for themselves, but for Him who died for them and rose again.

—2 CORINTHIANS 5:14–15

The Apostle Paul's life and service to the Lord provide a great example of jumping into the Christian life with both feet! However, a quick look at Paul's life shows that he immediately faced challenges as he followed the Lord. In just a matter of days after his conversion, some people were trying to kill him! Throughout Paul's life, he was faced with multiple attacks and never-ending criticism. Paul is an excellent example of what it means to live as one who is *called and accountable.*

The vigor he had when he jumped into the Christian life grew even more intense over his many years of service. Despite all of the hardships, he kept pressing forward with great strides. Have you ever wondered what gave Paul the power to stick to it—the power to continue to follow God? He stated plainly in 2 Corinthians 5:14 that *"the love of Christ"* compelled him—not his sense of duty or simply a stubborn personality, but his deep, abiding, growing love for Christ. This love had so radically impacted his life that he did not waver in his obedience to the Lord.

We know that God loves us, and we can read many Scriptures about God's love. In the Old Testament and New Testament, we see countless examples of God expressing His love to His people. But are we experiencing God's love in a real, practical, personal way? Is God's love bringing peace and a deep abiding joy into our lives? Is God's love bringing hope and a sense of purpose to our lives? If we recognize that the God of the universe is expressing His perfect love toward us, it will make a noticeable difference in our lives.

How can we know if we are experiencing this same love that compelled Paul? If we are, God's love is a compelling force in our lives, impacting everything we do. The more we release our lives to Christ and experience His love, the deeper our love for God grows. When we are compelled by God's love, we never tire of expressing His love to others.

Paul was often attacked, criticized, and shunned, yet he never stopped sharing God's love with the lost and with those in the church. Paul embraced God's love and released his life to experience the fullness of God's love. In turn, this love was the driving force in his life.

At times, we might tend to live out our Christian lives out of a sense of obligation, duty, or commitment. These are not bad things or motives, but, over time, they will become empty. Living our Christian lives compelled by the love of Christ will never result in emptiness.

Lord, I do love You, and I want the love that You have personally shown me to be the driving force in my life of service to You. Help me to be compelled by Your love and to develop a deep sense of stewardship to share Your love with a hurting world. Amen.

DIGGING DEEPER
THROUGH THE WEEK

Take time this week to read the following passages. As you read them, consider how the love of Christ compelled each person who encountered Jesus.

1. Luke 5:12–16

2. John 4:39–42

3. Luke 8:38–39

Accountable to Press On

Not that I have already attained, or am already perfected; but I press on, that I may lay hold of that for which Christ Jesus has also laid hold of me.

—Philippians 3:12

Sometimes we can become comfortable and too relaxed in our spiritual life. Complacency is dangerous as we become settled in our habits of Bible reading and prayer without recognizing that we are not growing or pressing on in obedience to the Lord. Looking at the Apostle Paul's life, we notice he was always striving to know more and experience more of what it meant to be a child of God.

Throughout the Book of Philippians, Paul charged the Philippian believers to live a life worthy of the gospel. Oftentimes he used his own life as an example. However, in Philippians 3:12, Paul admitted that he had not arrived. Many Christians quote Paul when they make a mistake or have a setback in their lives. In times of failure, we take comfort in the fact that we have not arrived yet, but are we taking the next step to *"press on"* so that we do not remain in the same place of failure? A time of failure is not a time to be discouraged, but an opportunity to press on so we don't wallow in self-pity, but turn our attention upward to God's next assignment.

What are we striving for in our lives? Paul's desire was to know Christ and to experience the wonders of a relationship with Christ. This pressing on gives the picture of an athlete running toward the finish line—it is not a passive description. If we don't actively press on, we will lose what we do have. We cannot attain the goal or finish the race by living a casual Christian life. Paul is an example of a man striving to grow in his walk with God. He had his eyes fixed on the goal.

How can we arrive at the goal? First, we must continually evaluate our lives and never assume we are OK in our Christian walk. Second, we must concentrate on the goal. A person who is running a race does not stop along the way to talk or admire the landscape. We must not allow ourselves to be caught up in things that distract us from the goal. Third, we must forget those things that are behind us. Persons who are always looking back are not likely to move forward. Finally, we must keep our eyes fixed on the goal: to walk worthy of the calling of God (Ephesians 4:1). If we take our eyes off Christ, we will lose our way.

 Heavenly Father, so many things in my life can cause me to take my focus off You. Please guide me today and in the coming week to follow You without missing one stride in this race. I love You, Lord! Amen.

DIGGING DEEPER
THROUGH THE WEEK

How would you describe your Christian life today? Could you say you have been pressing on like a runner looking toward the finish line? Are you pressing on to the goal for the prize of the upward call of God in Christ Jesus? Have you been sidetracked by your past failures or successes? None of us have arrived, but together, we press on to live a life worthy of the God who called us. Don't allow yourself to be sidetracked and miss out on what God intended for your race!

1. How have you been pressing on to walk worthy of the calling of God upon your life?

2. What evidence is there that you have been pressing on as opposed to standing still?

Topical Index

Scripture Reference Index

REFERENCES CITED BY DEVOTIONAL WEEK NUMBER

New Hope® Publishers is a division of WMU®,
an international organization that challenges Christian believers
to understand and be radically involved in God's mission.
For more information about WMU, go to www.wmu.com.
More information about New Hope books may be found
at www.newhopepublishers.com. New Hope books
may be purchased at your local bookstore.

BOOKS FOR MISSIONAL LIVING

Called and Accountable
*Discovering Your Place
in God's Eternal Purpose
(trade book)*
**Henry T. Blackaby and
Norman C. Blackaby**
ISBN-10: 1-59669-047-X
ISBN-13: 978-1-59669-047-9

Fueled by Faith
Living Vibrantly in the Power of Prayer
Jennifer Kennedy Dean
ISBN-10: 1-56309-993-4
ISBN-13: 978-1-56309-993-9

Directionally Challenged
*How to Find & Follow God's
Course for Your Life*
Travis Collins
ISBN-10: 1-59669-075-5
ISBN-13: 978-1-59669-075-2

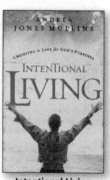

Intentional Living
Choosing to Live for God's Purposes
Andrea Jones Mullins
ISBN-10: 1-56309-927-6
ISBN-13: 978-1-56309-927-4

Available in bookstores everywhere
For information about these books or any New Hope®
product, visit www.newhopepublishers.com.